# THE
# ENOCHIAN
# EVOCATION
## OF
# DR. JOHN DEE

# THE
# ENOCHIAN
# EVOCATION
## OF
# DR. JOHN DEE

Edited and Translated by
Geoffrey James

WEISERBOOKS
San Francisco, CA / Newburyport, MA

This edition first published in 2009 by Weiser Books,
an imprint of Red Wheel/Weiser, LLC
With offices at:
500 Third Street, Suite 230
San Francisco, CA 94107
www.redwheelweiser.com

Previously published by Heptangle Books, Gillette, New Jersey, 1984 and by
Llewellyn Publications, St. Paul, Minnesota, as *The Enochian Magick of Dr. John
Dee* (1994).

ISBN: 978-1-57863-453-8

Library of Congress Cataloging-in-Publication Data available upon request.

Cover design by Dutton & Sherman Design
Typeset in Fournier MT text and Poor Richard display

Printed in the United States of America
MV
10 9 8 7 6 5 4 3 2 1

The paper used in this publication meets the minimum requirements of the Ameri-
can National Standard for Information Sciences-Permanence of Paper for Printed
Library Materials Z39.48-1992 (R1997).

# ACKNOWLEDGMENTS

I thank C.R. Runyon (of the Church of Hermetic Sciences) and David G. Kennedy for their assistance and criticism in the early stages of this project, and (especially) Daniel Driscoll for his patience, advice, and unstinting efforts to bring this volume to publication.

Magical sigils are reproduced by permission of the British Library.

*For Daniel Driscoll,*
*a visionary,*
*a kind man,*
*and a dear friend*
*who is sorely missed.*

# CONTENTS

# PREFACE TO THE WEISER EDITION

In the twenty-odd years since *The Enochian Evocation* was first published, I've come to realize that the book is more than I originally intended it to be.

My original intent was to create the grimoire that Dee never managed to complete on his own. I have no doubt that if Dee had intended others to replicate his angelic experiments, the text would have resembled this book.

I felt this was important because grimoires are a branch of religious literature that's virtually unstudied. Dee's actions represent the only historical record of how such literature is produced.

What you hold in your hands, then, is perhaps the only book about John Dee's magical work that, if Dee were still alive, he would be likely to completely understand and (probably) actively endorse. I tried to catch the "essence" of what Dee and Kelly were about, and think that, on the whole, I was successful.

Perhaps naively, I expected my book to be well-received by the scholarly community. Instead most of the interest in *The Enochian Evocation* has come (as far as I can tell) from practicing occultists. Academics have, by contrast, virtually ignored it.

The primary reason for the evident distaste among the ivy-covered professors is probably my assertion, in the original introduction, that the Angelic (aka Enochian) language has characteristics suggesting that it has non-human origins.

A completely new language that's non-human in origin. Yes, that's the kind of controversial statement that simply won't be tolerated among academics. I might as well clarify that statement, not for their benefit, but simply for the historical record.

While I believe that it's probable that the Angelic language was devised by somebody (most likely Kelly, either consciously or subconsciously), non-human characteristics do exist in the language and, as such, provide the best "proof" that we're ever likely to see of the existence of non-corporeal intelligence. Even if such beings are unlikely, Angelic is still the only example of Glossolalia (speaking in tongues) that involves a hitherto unknown language with its own grammar and syntax. This is a very different phenomenon from instances where entranced folk repeat languages that they might have heard when a child or, in the case of Pentecostal Christianity, spout whatever jibber-jabber comes into their heads.

In other words, this book is important because it's the only publication—scholarly or otherwise—that fairly assesses the unique and possibly significant phenomenon of the Angelic language and how it was dictated.

Think of it this way: either Angelic language represents proof of the existence of non-corporeal beings, or it does not. Either way, the mere existence of the Angelic language forces charismatic religious groups to a new standard of proof concerning the truth of their claims.

If somebody claims to be in touch with an angel or speaking for the "holy ghost," they should be able to communicate something at least as convincing as the Angelic language. If not, then their claims are obviously bogus or (as is more likely) the result of a purely subjective experience.

That being said, such issues are of small interest to the practicing occultist. Over the years, I've heard from several dozen practitioners for whom the existence of angelic beings is simply a fact of their day-to-day experience. For them, *The Enochian Evocation* is exactly what Dee would have wanted it to be: an instruction book for the practice of a uniquely powerful form of magic. Which is, of course, exactly what I originally intended it to be as well.

*Geoffrey James*
*Addis Ababa*

# PREFACE

## Geoffrey James

THE ENOCHIAN EVOCATION is based on the magical diaries & workbooks of Doctor John Dee, the famous Elizabethan scientist and magus. These manuscripts document the ceremonies that Dee performed with Edward Kelly, who, gazing into a crystal stone, claimed to see and hear angels. According to Kelly, these beings desired to re-establish the true art of Magic, which had been lost due to Man's wickedness and ignorance. The true magical art (they claimed) would bequeath superhuman powers upon its practitioners, change the political structure of Europe, and herald the coming of the Apocalypse.

Dee believed that this research was of great benefit to Mankind and far more important than his more mundane studies. Dee explained his dissatisfaction with worldly knowledge:

> *I have from my youth up, desired and prayed unto God for pure and sound wisdom and understanding of truths natural and artificial, so that God's wisdom, goodness, and power bestowed in the frame of the world might be brought in some bountiful measure under the talent of my capacity... So for many years and in many places, far and near, I have sought and studied many books in sundry languages, and have conferred with sundry men, and have laboured with my own reasonable discourse, to find some inkling, gleam, or beam of those radical truths. But after all my endeavours I could find no other way to attain such wisdom but by the Extraordinary Gift, and not by any vulgar school, doctrine, or human invention.\**

Dee felt that only through the practice of magic would he be able to learn those 'radical truths.' Like Luther, Dee rejected the necessity of the church as an intermediary to God. But Dee carried this doctrine one step further, believing that holy revelations

---

\* From Dee's Preface to Sloane MS. 3188.

2A

could be obtained by practicing the magic of the ancient Hebrews:

*I had read in books and records how Enoch enjoyed God's favor and conversation, and how God was familiar with Moses, and how good angels were sent to Abraham, Isaac, Jacob, Joshua, Gideon, Esdras, Daniel, Tobias, and sundry others, to instruct them, inform them and help them in worldly and domestic affairs, and even sometimes to satisfy their desires, doubts, and questions of God's secrets. Furthermore, I considered the Shewstone which the high priests did use, by God's own ordering, wherein they had lights and judgements in their great doubts. I considered, too, that God did not refuse to instruct the prophets and seers to give answers to the common people concerning economics, as Samuel did for Saul; and so did Solomon the wise, immediately after attaining his wonderful wisdom through God. Therefore I was sufficiently taught and confirmed that I would never attain wisdom by man's hand or by human power, but only from God, directly or indirectly.†*

Realizing the heretical aspects of these beliefs at a time when magic was perceived as questionable at best and at worst diabolic, Dee was vehement in his rejection of the 'black arts':

*I have always had a great regard and care to beware of the filthy abuse of such as willingly or wittingly invoke or consult with spiritual creatures of the damned sort: angels of darkness, forgers, patrons of lies and untruths. Instead I have flown unto God through hearty prayer, full oft and in sundry manners.‡*

Dee discovered that he was unable to perceive spirits on his own, and so was forced to employ skryers or crystal gazers. The most prolific of Dee's skryers was Edward Kelly, a man of mediocre education whose main interest was alchemy. Kelly originally asked to work with Dee because Kelly believed that with divine aide they might discover the philosopher's stone that would transmute lead into gold. Dee was hesitant at first, but when they performed a simple ceremony, it was far more successful than anything Dee had ever experienced:

† *Ibidem*
‡ *Ibidem*

*Thereupon I brought forth to him my stone in the frame (which was given me of a friend) and I said unto him, that I was credibly informed that to it (after a sort) were answerable various good Angels . . . He then settled himself to the Action: and on his knees at my desk, setting the stone before him, fell to prayer and entreaty. In the mean space, I in my oratory did pray and make motion to God & his good Creatures for the furthering of this Action. And within a quarter of an hour (or less) he had sight of one in the stone.\**

Kelly's skrying was destined to produce what is perhaps the most unusual magical literature of the Renaissance.

Was Kelly a charlatan who fabricated visions out of his own imagination ? Historians have traditionally cast Kelly as a *fraud who deluded his pious master*†, but the evidence perhaps does not justify this judgement. It is true that Kelly accepted £50 per year for his services to Dee‡ but such annuities were the basis for survival in Elizabethan times. Far from encouraging Dee, Kelly eventually began to question the angelic nature of the spirits, and frequently tried to extricate himself from Dee's employ⁂. Kelly might, of course, have been applying reverse psychology, but there is little reason why he should have bothered to do so, as Dee was already determined to continue the experimentation. If Kelly had been trying to plunder Dee's money, why would Kelly have tried to convince Dee that the spirits were devils ?

It is difficult to account for the serious stylistic differences between Kelly's usual writing style and the utterances that he attributed to the spirits. Kelly was an uninspired writer; the following exerpt is representative of his prowess:

*The heavenly cope hath in him nature's fower*
*Two hidden, but the rest to sight appear:*
*Wherein the sperms of all the bodies lower*
*Most secrett are, yett spring forth once a yeare...*§

* Sloane MS. 3188; Passages marked March 10, 1582.
† Francis Yates, *Gordiano Bruno and the Hermetic Tradition*, London: 1964, p. 149.
‡ Meric Casaubon, ed., *A True and Faithful Relation of What passed for many Yeers Between Dr. John Dee . . . and some Spirits*, London: 1659, pg. 28. (Facsimilie republished by Askin, London: 1974.)
⁂ *Ibidem*, pgs. 20, 91, 153, 169 & 171.
§ A. E. Waite, ed., *The Alchemical Writings of Edward Kelly*, Weiser, New York: 1973, p. liii.

Contrast those stilted and awkward lines with the Call of the Thirty Aires:

> *The work of man and his pomp,*
> *let them be defaced:*
> *His buyldings*
> *Let them become caves for the beasts of the fiield:*
> *Confownd her understanding with darkness.*
> *For why?*
> *It repenteth me I made Man.*

It seems impossible that this powerful passage could have been written by the same hand, or that Kelly's own writing skill could have produced such passages of eldrich beauty as:

> *Can the wings of the windes understand your voyces of wonder?...*
> *Stronger are your fete than the barren stone:*
> *And mightier are your voices than the manifold windes....*

Admittedly, stylistic differences are subtle gauges of authorship. But more concrete evidence against Kelly fabricating all his visions lies in the complexity of the Angelical (Enochian) keys. Could Kelly, whose single linguistic accomplishment was mastery of schoolboy Latin and even whose English was laced with colloquialisms, have devised an entire language, with its own unique grammar and syntax? It took Tolkien, a professor of philology, years to fabricate the Elvish tongue that figures so largely in his work; if Kelly fabricated the keys, he would have had to do so in a matter of days.

In short, if Kelly was the conscious author of all his 'visions', then he possessed a far greater literary competence than he ever exhibited elsewhere. However, the subconscious mind is often capable of feats that are impossible to the conscious mind. Could Kelly have hallucinated the visions? It has been suggested that Dee may have propelled Kelly into a state of artificial psychosis with their ceremonies.† Kelly may also have had multiple personalities, for the spirits talk in biblical dialects quite different from Kelly's normal speech.

† Peter French, *John Dee, The World of the Elizabethian Magus*, London: Routledge & Kegan Paul, 1972, pg. 114.

Kelly was having trouble distinguishing between his own thoughts and those of the 'spirits'. He complained of :

*...a great stir and moving in his brains, very sensible and distinct, as of a creature of human shape and lineaments going up and down, to and fro in his brains and within his skull.‡*

Dee was forcing Kelly to perform ceremonies on an almost daily basis, and for hours at a stretch. Reflecting this stress, Kelly's temper became extremely volatile as shown by this event that Dee recorded:

*Suddenly E. K. fell into such a rage that...much ado I, Emericus, and his brother had to stop or hold him...At length we let him go in his doublet and hose, without a cap or hat on his head: and into the street he hastened with his brother's rapier drawn... The rage and fury was so great in words and gesture as might plainly prove that the wicked enemy sought either E. K. his own destroying himself, or of me, or of his brother.***

Kelly's behaviour was so bizarre that Dee was afraid that Kelly was possessed by the devil, one of the time's standard diagnoses for insanity. Dee had recently discovered that Kelly was performing black magic independent of their work together. This horrified Dee so much that he noted the event in Latin, even in his own private diary:

*Horrenda & multiplicia heresium, & blasphemiarum dogmata, quibus illi hostes Jesu Christi illum imbuerant...illisque malis Angelis renunciare, & omnes illorum fraudes deteger... Conversio E. K. ad Deum, abdicatis omnibus Diabolicis experimentis.§*

The 'horrible heresies' that the 'evil angels' had revealed to Kelly were, in the context of the time, insane. They questioned the entire fabric on which the culture was built. Dee recorded these heresies in his diary:

‡ Casaubon, *op. cit.*, p. 328.
*** *Ibidem*, p. 230.
§ *Ibidem*, p. 164: Manifold horrible heresies and blasphemous doctrines, in which they eat the host of Jesus Christ ... but he was led to put aside these evil angels and all their frauds. . . I spoke with E. K. about God, telling him to give over all his Diabolical experiments.

*They would have persuaded (Kelly):*
*—That Jesus was not God.*
*—That no prayer ought to be made to Jesus.*
*—That there is no sin.*
*—That man's soul doth go from one body to another childes quickening*
*—That as many men and women as are now, have always been.*
*—That the generation of mankind from Adam and Eve, is not an History, but a writing which has another sense.**

Kelly could not have entertained such notions without being profoundly disturbed by their implications, and his conversion back to orthodoxy indicates his remorse and guilt. There is little question that Kelly was exhibiting signs of extreme stress and possible psychosis while working with Dee.

Kelly's participation in private magical ceremonies raises the tantalizing possibility that he might have had access to magical texts of which Dee was not aware, and that may have served as source material for the *Enochian Evocation*. Although Israel Regardie states that *there is absolutely no trace of any part of the Enochian magical system or Angelical language in Europe.*†; that viewpoint is not entirely justified. While it is true that the Angelical keys are very different from, for example, the bastardized Arabic and Greek in various Solomonic grimoires, elements of the *Enochian Evocation* are similar and in some cases almost identical to other Renaissance magical texts.

Both the *Arbatel*‡ and the *Heptameron*‡ are arranged like Book Two of the *Enochian Evocation*, with conjurations addressed to the rulers of each day of the week. The sigil of Æmeth, also in Book Two, is apparently based upon an earlier sigil that appears in the *Sworn Book of Honourius*,§ a manuscript that antedated Kelly by almost 300 years. Of course, the entire methodology for devising spirit sigils out of magical squares of numbers and or letters was described in detail by Cornelius Agrippa *c.* 1533.**

* *loc, cit.*
† Israel Regardie, *The Golden Dawn*, St. Paul: Llewellyn, 1971, p. 208.
‡ Anonymous, *Arbatel, De Magia Verum*, Basileæ: 1575; or Robert Turner, tr., Gillette: Heptangle Books, 1979.
‡ Henrici Cornelii Agrippæ, *Liber Quartus De Occulta Philosophia seu de Ceremoniis Magicis Cui accessurunt Elementa Magica Petri de Abano Philosophi*, Location not given, 1565; or Robert Turner, tr., *Fourth Book of the Occult Philosophy*, London: 1655; (Facsimile by Askin, London: 1974.)
§ Daniel Driscoll, tr., *The Sworn Book of Honourius the Magician*, Gillette: Heptangle Books, 1977.
** *De Occulta Philosophia*, Sine loco, 1533.

Renaissance Europe did contain books of evocation magic attributed to Enoch. The very year the keys were dictated, Reginald Scot complained:

> *Conjurors carrie about at this daie, bookes intitled under the names of Adam, Abel, Tobie, & Enoch; which Enoch they repute the most divine fellow in such matters\**.

Could Kelly have been utilizing such a book to assist him in his private ceremonies, or to provide the material that Dee so incessantly demanded? Kelly was certainly guilty of some plagiarism, although it may have been subconscious, for it was Kelly rather than Dee, who discovered the plagiarism and reported it to Dee:

> *(Kelly) came speedily out of his Study, and brought in his hand one volume of Cornelius Agrippa his works... whereupon he inferred, that our spiritual Instructors were Cosenors to give us a description of the world, taken out of other Books...†*

Dee, somewhat surprised, replied: *I am very glad that you have a Book of your own, wherein these Geographical names are expressed‡*. Dee's ignorance of the exact contents of the library that Kelly kept in his study is extremely suspicious.

If Kelly was plagiarizing some as-yet undiscovered manuscript, it may have been Gnostic in origin, as significant parallels exist between the Angelical keys and certain Gnostic texts. For example, a typical incantation from the *Pistis Sophia:* ZAMA ZAMA OZZA RACHAMA OZAI‡ is not Angelical, but the overuse of the 'Z' phoneme is characteristic of Angelical, and the repetition of the word ZAMA echoes the refrain ZACAR CA ZAMRAN that permeates the keys. Another linguistic similarity is the Gnostic name for the demiurge IALDABAOTH,§ quite close to the Angelical IAD BALTOH for 'God of Righteousness.'

The Gnostics tended to treat Enoch as a special personage, because he was the first mortal to speak with God after the fall,

---

\* Reginald Scot, *The Discovery of Witchcraft*, London: William Brome, 1584, Book xv, Chapter xxxi.

† Casaubon, *op. cit.*, p. 158.

‡ *Ibidem.*

‡ G. R. S. Mead, *Fragments of a Faith Forgotton*, New York: University Books, 1960, p. 462.

§ *Ibidem*, p. 188.

and so the first to attain the gnosis that they sought§. The Gnostics attributed works of magic to Enoch, such as *the two great Books of* IEOU, *which Enoch wrote when I spoke with him from the Tree of Knowledge, which were in the paradise of Adam**. The word IEOU suggests that the books contained conjurations with words much like those of the *Pistis Sophia* or the Angelical keys; the legendary origin of the Books in the garden of Eden recalls the claim that the Angelical language was that *which Adam verily spake in innocence*.

Like many Gnostic texts, the Angelical keys emphasize the opening of 'gates' into various mystical realms. The *Book of the Great Logos*, a Gnostic text associated with the Books of IEOU, contains the following passage:

> *The guardians of the Gates of the treasure will open them, and they will pass upwards and ever inwards through the following spaces, and the powers rejoicing and giving them their mysteries, seals, and names of power: the Orders of the Three Amens...Within each treasure is a Door or Gate, and without three Gates; each of the outer gates has three guardians.*†

Compare the above passage with the following from Kelly's scrying:

> *Every table hath his key, every key openeth his gate, and every gate being opened, giveth knowledge of himself, of the entrance, and the mysteries of those things whereof he is an enclosure. Within these Palaces you shall find things that are of power...for every Palace is above his City and every City is above his Entrance.*‡

Both Gnostic and Angelical magic place emphasis on the number 49. For example, the *Pistis Sophia* states that *the reflection of the supernal projections, powers, or co-partners of the Sophia [when] looked at from without, make an ordering into forty-nine,*⁑ while the apoc-

§ *Vide: The Secrets of Enoch*, published in *The Lost Books of the Bible*, Cleveland: Forum Books, 1963.
* Mead, *op. cit.*, p. 487.
† *Ibidem*, p. 258 & 541.
‡ Casaubon, *op. cit.*, p. 88.
⁑ Mead, *op. cit.*, p. 471.

ryphal *Books of the Savior* state that *no mystery is higher than the mysteries ye seek after, save only the mystery of the Seven Voices and the Nine-and-Forty Powers and Numbers.*\* These 49 powers recall the 49 good angels or even the Angelical keys themselves, which Kelly's spirits described as:

> *49 voyces , or callings, which are the Natural Keys, to open...Gates of understanding...you shall have knowledge to move every Gate, and to call out as many as you please...and wisely open unto you the secrets of their Cities...*†

The possibility that Kelly did plagiarize large portions of the *Enochian Evocation* would do much to explain the presence of the Angelical language in his scrying, as well as the stylistic variations in his work. However, the similarity between Kelly's scrying and Gnostic magic, while undeniable, is not sufficiently strong to build a direct textual connection.

A serious objection to the theory that Kelly plagiarized visions is the way that the keys were revealed. The first five keys were dictated, letter by letter, backwards, while the rest were dictated forwards, without any significant errors. The bulk of the keys (over 1000 words) were dictated on a single day during a single session. Most of the English glosses were dictated on a single day, well after the Angelical, yet they match their Angelical counterparts almost perfectly. Kelly would have had to be capable of extraordinary feats of mnemonic virtuosity, if he utilized another magical text as source material for the keys.

A final possibility deserves discussion—was Kelly ever actually in contact with supernatural entities? In fact, the Dee-Kelly ceremonies contain some evidence that would seem to indicate the presence of the supernatural during some of the ceremonies.

One standard test for the presence of the supernatural is precognition of future events. This took place at least twice during the Dee-Kelly workings; the spirits predicted the Spanish armada and the execution of Mary Queen of Scots well before those events could have been known.‡ However, the 'spirits' predicted other events that never took place.

---

\* *Ibidem*, pgs. 516 & 523.

† Casaubon, *op. cit.*, p. 77.

‡ Donald C. Laycock, *The Complete Enochian Dictionary*, London: Askin, 1978, p. 38

Another classic test for the presence of the supernatural is the speaking of a tongue with which the possessed is not familiar. During one ceremony, Kelly began repeating Greek words, but he soon became frustrated and interrupted with: *Unless you speak some language that I can understand, I will express no more of this Ghybbrish*§. Curiously, the Greek translates into a warning to Dee not to trust Kelly.

But the Angelical language itself forms a more startling example of 'speaking in tongues', because it exhibits characteristics that would seem to indicate that it was designed to be a non-spoken language. As Da Vinci had pointed out nearly 100 years before the keys were dictated, spirits would be unable to make audible sounds on their own, due to a lack of vocal chords with which to vibrate the air*.

Thus any 'language' that spirits would 'speak' would be radically different from a language intended for use by human beings. Onomatapœiæ would be totally lacking. Contractions would be used to create new concepts, rather than to smooth out pronunciation. Many words would feature strings of consonants rather than an easily-pronounced intermixes of vowels and consonants. The letter arrangement would appear somewhat random and more like a Cabbala than a spoken tongue. And finally, the system of numbers would not be based on 10, since along with a lack of vocal chords, non-material entities would have little use for fingers.

The Angelical language exhibits most of these characteristics. There are no onomatapeioæ in Angelical. Angelical contractions such as TELOCVOVIM and JADOIASMOMA are conceptually convenient, but have not been edited for easier pronunciation. Many Angelical words feature unpronounceable strings of consonants. Angelical letter arrangements appear to be random‡, and the language is stated to be the source language for Hebrew and thus Cabbala is implied. Finally, Angelical numbers are incomprehensible using any known base or numbering scheme‡.

§ Casaubon, *op. cit.*, p. 27.
* Jean Paul Richter, tr., *The Notebooks of Leonardo Da Vinci*, New York: Dover Publications, 1970, Vol. II, p. 307.
‡ Laycock, *op. cit.*, p. 40.
‡ *Ibidem*, p. 44.

The compiler of the Enochian dictionary, on the other hand, asserts that the Angelical language is English-like both in word order and in pronunciation. Since the exact character of the Angelical language is essential to an understanding of *The Enochian Evocation*, Laycock's theory must be examined in some detail.

Laycock gives an example where English is the only language that matches the Angelical§. But the keys include many other passages where the Angelical phrasing makes for extremely awkward English. For example, Niiso Crip Ip Nidali is glossed as *Come awaye, but not your noyses*. Since this is addressed to the *Thunderers of Judgement and Wrath*, what is probably meant by Niiso Crip Ip Nidali is *leave wherever you are and come here, but don't make thundering noises*. The Angelical language expresses the concept much more succinctly than is possible in English. Again, the Angelical word Telocvovim is glossed as *him that is faln [fallen]*, but is actually a contraction of Teloch (death) and Vovin (dragon), literally 'death-dragon'—a reference to Satan's transformation during his fall. Words like Telocvovim are much more Germanic than English-like. In short, the Angelical language is no more English-like than any other non-English language; the fact that there are some matches is not significant.

Laycock states that the Angelical language has English pronunciations. Unfortunately, Kelly never, as the spirits' 'mouthpiece', pronounced the Angelical words. Kelly dictated letter by letter from a table that he saw in the crystal, as shown from Kelly's description that Dee recorded:

> [*The angel*] *hath a rod or wand in his hand...it is of Gold...He standeth upon his round table of Christal or rather Mother of Pearl: There appear an infinite number of letters on the same, as thick as can stand by another...He standeth and pointeth with his rod to the letters of his Table, as if he made some account or reckoning‡.*

Furthermore, if Angelical letter arrangement has random characteristics, as Laycock claims, then the English-like pronunciation cannot be an inherent quality of the language itself. Far more likely is that Dee assigned pronunciations to the Angelical because

§ *Ibidem*, p. 43.
‡ Casaubon, *op. cit.*, p. 73.

he wished to speak the keys in a ceremony, and, being English, adapted them as well as he could to his native tongue. Indeed, outside of few minor suggestons, the spirits seem unconcerned with pronunciation. The Angelical language in its basic form makes few concessions to the human vocal chord.

Of course, one' must keep in mind that Kelly might have plagiarized the keys; in any case, whoever or whatever devised the keys made a viable attempt to simulate a 'language' designed for non-material beings.

The final and most dramatic evidence for the presence of the supernatural is a telekinetic phenomenon that Dee himself witnessed and described:

> *There appeared a great flame of fire in the principal Stone....Suddenly one seemed to come in at the fourth window of the Chappel... the stone was heaved up a handful high and set down again. The one at the window seemed... with spread-abroad arms to come to E. K., at which sight, he shrinked back somewhat, and then that Creature took up between both his hands the stone and frame of gold, and mounted up away as he came E. K. catched at it, but he could not touch it ...E. K. was in a great fear and trembling and had* tremorem cordis *for a while. But I was very glad and well pleased\*.*

Although it is true that this event could easily be reproduced using modern techniques of prestidigitation, stage magic in the 16th century was much too crude to produce such an illusion†. If Kelly had some trick of making a crystal rise and fly out a window, he could have made far more than £50 a year performing this feat for the public. Kelly's reaction to the event is revealing; Dee apparently listened to his heart and noticed tremors, a condition that Kelly would have found difficult to simulate. Kelly seems genuinely affected, but the cold and clinical Dee declared that he was *glad and well pleased.* The event proved to Dee, beyond the shadow of all doubt, that they were in contact with supernatural powers.

* \* *Ibidem*, Second page 19.
* † *Vide*, Scot, *op. cit.*, Book XIII, Chapter xxxiv, for a description of the primitive stage illusions of the 16th Century.

Was Kelly a charlatan, a psychotic, a plagiarist, or a true skryer? The distinction was non-existent in Kelly's own mind, because differentiating between these states required a well-defined sense of reality. There is no simple explanation for Kelly's actions. He believed in the spirits, yet he fabricated and plagiarized. He exhibited the signs of psychosis, yet manifested extraordinary linguistic and telekinetic phenomena. Forced on an almost daily basis into abnormal psychological and hypnotic states, plagued by the constant fear of damnation, convinced to let his life be controlled by 'angels' that were either manifestations of his diseased subconscious or of strange otherworldly presences–all these served to blur Kelly's perception of reality.

It is ironic that Kelly is so often viewed as victimizing Dee. Kelly was forced to stay with Dee because the money that the doctor gave him supported Kelly's wife and brother. When Kelly tried to leave, Dee would coerce him to remain by playing on his guilt and fear. It was Dee, not Kelly, who was gaining the benefit from the magical ceremonies, for it sated his lust for 'radical truths'.

A single incident epitomizes the difference between the attitudes of the two men. The spirits demanded that Dee and Kelly have sexual relations with each other's wives. Whether the suggestion came from Kelly's subconscious or from some other source is not important; what is important is the reactions of the two men.

Kelly was appalled and, in a rare lucid moment, insisted that Dee include a written protest in his magical diaries:

*I, Edward Kelly, by good and provident determination and consideration in these former Actions, that is to say, appearings, shews made, and voyces uttered...have from the beginning thereof (which at large by the records appeareth) not only doubted and disliked their insinuations and doctrine but also at diverse and sundry times... sought to depart from the exercises thereof...they manifestly [have] urged and commanded in the name of God a Doctrine Damnable and contrary to the Laws of God.\**

\* Casaubon, *op. cit.*, Second page 17.

Dee had his own doubts, and for the first time calls the spirits 'apparitions'‡. But Dee was not willing to admit that the 'radical truths' might have had a less than divine origin, and, against all the protests of Kelly and the two wives (who 'disliked utterly this last doctrine'), Dee drew up an elaborate contract that included the following stipulation:

> *this doctrine and doings should unto no mortal man be disclosed, but among us onely the above-named four to be kept most secret... we all and every four of us do request...that the sudden and immediate death may light and fall onto the discloser and on him or her to whom the same doctrine or doing any manner of way shall be disclosed or known*‡*.

Thus the hypocritical Dee was willing to pretend that he was following the commandments of God, but asked for death for anyone who found out about it.

The ceremonies continued for some time, possibly pushing Kelly beyond the limits of sanity. After splitting with Dee, he foolishly proclaimed (and perhaps believed himself) that he had indeed discovered the Philosopher's Stone. Finally, in another manic rage, he murdered a man and was imprisoned for the rest of his life. When finally given the opportunity to escape from his tower prison, he fell (or jumped?) to his death§.

Dee felt no guilt for any of his magical experiments, and continually protested his own innocence of any wrongdoing:

> *The great losses and damages which I have sustained do not grieve my heart so much as the rash, lewd, fond, and most untrue fables and reports of me and my philosophical studies... The works of my hands and the words of my mouth bear lively witness to the thoughts of my heart and inclination of my mind*§§.

Even in the last years of his life, Dee was willing to stand trial for Witchcraft, convinced that even the repressive courts under

‡ *Ibidem*, Second page 13.
* *Ibidem*, Second page 21.
§ A.E. Waite, *Alchemists Through the Ages*, New York, Steiner,1970,p.158
§§ Casaubon, *op cit*, Dee's Apology to the Archbishop of Canterbury.

James the First would acquit him.*

Dee's quest was a spiritual one and his sincere intention was to bring God's wisdom to Mankind. Dee tried to extend the power of Man beyond the threshold of science. While Dee's fanaticism and blind faith in the reality of Kelly's skrying caused others to suffer, one must admit that Dee himself did not escape unscathed. Once the news of his magical practices had become public knowledge, his house and belongings were partially destroyed by a mob of ignorant peasants. And despite the spirits' promises of vast treasures, Dee died in abject poverty, still practicing magic to the end of his days.†

*The Enochian Evocation* reveals those magical arts, those 'radical truths' for which Doctor John Dee, the foremost scientist and magus of his time, risked his reputation, the virtue of his wife, the sanity of his friend, and the salvation of his own soul.

GEOFFREY JAMES

LOS ANGELES,

AUGUST, 1982.

* French, *op. cit.*, p. 10.
† Laycock, *op. cit.*, p. 53.

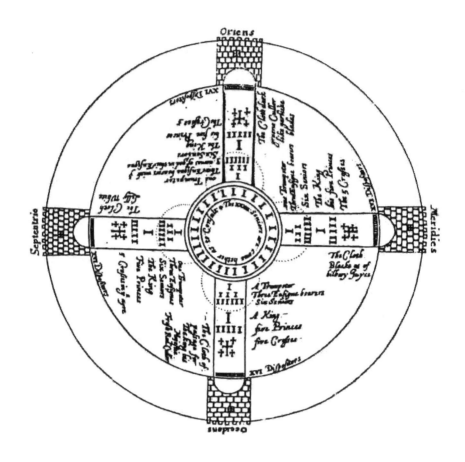

## THE GOLDEN TALISMAN

[*Vide:* APPENDIX A, ¶V., p. 187–88.]

# BOOK ONE

# THE MAGICK OF ENOCH

ᛥ ᛥ ᛥ

CHAPTER I.

## THE FALL OF MAN

§1. *The Garden of Eden.*

AN, IN HIS CREATION, BEING MADE AN INNOCENT, WAS also authorized and made partaker of the Power and Spirit of God. He not only knew all things under Creation and spoke of them properly— naming them as they were—but was also a partaker of the presence and society of Angels, a speaker of the mysteries of God, and spoke even with God Himself. ᛥ So in that innocence, the power of his partaking with God and His good Angels was exalted, and so became holy in the sight of God.

§2. *The Casting Out of Adam.*

ᛥBut Coronzon (for so is the name of that mighty devil), envying man's felicity, and perceiving that the substance of man's lesser part was frail and unperfect in respect to his purer essence, began to assail man, and so prevailed. By offending so, man became accursed in the sight of God, and so lost both the Garden of Felicity and the judgement of his understanding, but not utterly the favor of God. But he was driven forth (as your scriptures record) unto the Earth which was covered with brambles. ᛥAdam received punishment for his offence, in that he was turned out into the earth, and so did Adam, accursed, bring all misery and wretchedness into the world. But in the same instant when Adam was expelled, the Lord gave unto the world her

I

A

time, and placed over her Angelic Keepers, Watchmen, and Princes.

§3. *The Origin of Hebrew.*

Being as dumb, and not able to speak, Adam began to learn (through necessity) the language which thou callest Hebrew but not in the form which is now Hebrew amongst you. Adam uttered and delivered to his posterity the nearest knowledge that he had of God and His Creatures. From his own self, he divided this speech into three parts: twelve, three, and seven. This division yet remaineth, but the true forms and pronunciations are lost. Therefore Hebrew is not of that force that it was in its original dignity; much less is it to be compared with this language that we deliver, which Adam verily spake in innocence and which has never been uttered nor disclosed to man since, until now. In this language, the power of God must work and wisdom in her true kind must be delivered.

# THE WISDOM OF ENOCH.

### §1. *The Lord & Enoch.*

THEN THE LORD APPEARED UNTO ENOCH AND WAS merciful unto him and opened up his eyes so that he might see and judge the earth, which was unknown unto his parents by reason of their fall. For the Lord said: *Let us show unto Enoch the use of the earth.* And lo, Enoch was wise and full of the spirit of wisdom.

### §2. *The Prayer of Enoch.*

*Thrice a day did Enoch talk with God, and this was his prayer:*

CAN THE VESSEL OF FEAR, FRAGILITY, OR THAT WHICH IS OF A determined proportion, lift up himself, heave up his hands, and gather the sun into his bosom? Lord, it cannot be. Lord, my imperfection is great. Lord, I am less than sand. Lord, thy good Angels and Creatures excel me by far, for our proportion is not alike and our senses agreeth not.

Notwithstanding I am comforted. For we all have one God, all one beginning from thee, and all respect thee as Creator. Therefore I will call upon thy name and in thee I will become mighty. Thou shalt light me, and I will become a Seer. I will see thy Creatures and will magnify thee amongst them.

Those that come into thee have the same gate, and through that same gate descend those that thou sendest. Behold, I will offer my house, my labour, my heart and soul, if it will please thy Angels to dwell with me and I with them—to rejoice with me that I might rejoice with them—to minister unto me that I might magnify thy name.

Aa

Then, lo, these Tables (which I have provided and prepared according to thy will) I offer unto thee and unto thy holy Angels, desiring them through thy holy Names. As thou art their light and comfort, so they will be my light and comfort. Lord, they prescribe no laws unto thee, thus it is not meet that I prescribe laws unto them. What it pleases them to offer unto me, I will receive. Behold, Oh Lord, if I shall call them in thy name, be it unto me in mercy, as unto the servant of the Highest. Let them manifest unto me, howsoever I shall call them and at whatever time.

Oh Lord, is there any who is mortal that can measure the heavens? How, therefore, can the heavens enter into man's Imagination? Thy Creatures are the glory of thy countenance and thereby thou glorifiest all things; but this glory excelleth and is far above my understanding. It is great wisdom to speak with Kings according to one's understanding, but to command Kings is not wisdom unless it come from thee.

Behold, Lord, how shall I ascend into the heavens? The air will not carry me, but resisteth my folly. I fall down, for I am of the earth. Therefore, oh thou very light and true comfort, that canst command the Heavens: Behold, I offer these Tables unto thee. Command them as it pleaseth thee. Oh you Ministers and true lights of understanding, who govern this earthly frame and the elements wherein we live: Do for me as for the servant of the Lord. For unto me it has pleased the Lord to talk of you.

Behold, Lord, thou hast appointed me 50 times. Thrice 50 times I will lift up my hands unto thee. Be it unto me as it pleaseth thee and thy holy Ministers. I require nothing but thee, through thee, and for thy honor and glory. Yet I hope that I shall be satisfied and shall not die (as thou hast promised) until thou gatherest the clouds together to judge all things. And in that moment I shall be changed and dwell with thee forever.

§3. *The Book of Enoch.*

⅜And at the end of the 50 days, there appeared unto Enoch that which is not now to be manifested nor spoken of. Enoch enjoyed the fruit of God, his promise, and received the benefit of his faith. Here may the wise learn wisdom; for what doth man do that is not corruptible? ⅜And Enoch said unto the Lord: *Let there by remembrance of thy mercy, and let those that love thee taste of this after me. Oh let not thy mercy be forgotten.* And the Lord was pleased. So after 50 days, Enoch wrote, and this was the title of his books: LET THOSE THAT FEAR GOD AND ARE WORTHY —READ.

CHAPTER IIJ

# THE FALL OF ENOCH'S MAGICK.

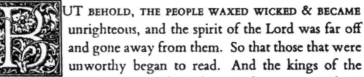

### §1. *The Unworthy Read Enoch's Book.*

UT BEHOLD, THE PEOPLE WAXED WICKED & BECAME unrighteous, and the spirit of the Lord was far off and gone away from them. So that those that were unworthy began to read. And the kings of the earth said thus against the Lord: *What is it that we cannot do, & who is he that can resist us?*

### §2. *The Lord Sends Wicked Spirits.*

And the Lord was vexed, and he sent in amongst them 150 lions, spirits of wickedness, error, and deceit. And they appeared unto the kings of the earth, for the Lord had put them between those that are wicked and his good Angels. And these spirits began to counterfeit the doings of God and His power, for they had power given to them to do so. And the memory of Enoch washed away.

### §3. *Enoch's Magick Forgotten.*

The knowledge of mystical figures and their use is the gift of God delivered unto Enoch and (by Enoch's request) unto the faithful, that they might have the true use of God's Creatures, and of the earth whereon they dwell. So hath the Devil delivered unto the wicked the signs and tokens of his error and hatred towards God, so that they, in using them, might consent in their will and so become partakers with him in his reward, which is æternal damnation. These signs they call Characters—a lamentable thing—for by these many souls have perished. For the doings of the Ægyptians seem, but are not so. The doings of the Lord are, and continue to be. But, as the painter imitates the gestures of man, so doth the Devil imitate the substance and things created and made by God.

6

§4. *Concerning Satan.*

Where are the monuments that Satan hath built? Hath he not built a fort on the whole earth? Hath he not victory over the Saints? Dwelleth he not in the temple of the Highest? Triumpheth he not in the cities of the world? But without comfort are his victories and without pleasure are his dwelling places, for he knoweth that his time is at hand. He that now hath freedom shall become bound. He unto whom the whole world is a garden, there shall not be one foot left. Therefore are all his pleasures vanity, all his triumphs smoke, and his authority nothing but a meer shadow.

## CHAPTER IV

# THE REESTABLISHMENT OF ENOCH'S WISDOM.

§1. *The Lord is Displeased With Man.*

THE GODHEAD, KEEPING IN HIS ALMIGHTY BOSOM THE image and form of all things, looked down upon the earth, and said: *Let us now go down amongst the sons of men.* But he saw that all things grew contrary to their creation and nature, either keeping their dignities and secret virtue shut up in obscurity, or else riotously perishing through imbecility and ignorance.

So then he said: *Behold, I delight not in the World. The Elements are defiled. The sons of men are wicked, their bodies are become dunghills, and the inward parts (which are the secret chambers of their hearts) are become the dens and dungeons of the damned. Therefore, I will draw my spirit from amongst them, and they shall become more drunken, and their ignorance shall become such as never was before...no, not since the fall of the heavens ! For, Lo, the time is come, and he that is the Son of the Unrighteousness liveth. Unto him shall be given strength and power. The kings of the earth shall become mad, yea, even raging mad, yea, even unto the third madness in the depth of their own imagination. But I will build my temple in the woods and in the desert places and will become a serpent in the wilderness.*

§2. *The Lord Relenteth.*

Lo, the Thunder spake, and the earth became misty and full of fog, so that the soul of man might sleep in its own confusion. The second Thunder spake, and there arose spirits, such as are for Soothsayers, Witches, Charmers, and Seducers. They have entered into the holy places and have taken up their seats in man.

Woe be unto the earth, for she is corrupted. Woe be unto the earth, for she is surrendered to her adversary. Woe be unto the earth, for she is delivered into the hands of her enemy. Yea, woe be unto the sons of man, for their vessels are poisoned. But even then said the Lord: *I will be known in the wilderness and will Triumph in my weakness.*

§3. *The Lord Sends Raphæl to Dee & Kelly.*

**55**And lo, he called you. And you became drunken and foolish with the spirit of God. The Lord said: *Descend, for he calleth.* And so Raphæl (who had brought up your prayer) descended, and he was full of the power and spirit of God. And he delivered a Doctrine—neither painted nor carved nor imagined by man—but simple, plain, full of strength and the power of the Holy Ghost. This doctrine began, as man did, nakedly from the earth, but is yet the image of perfection. It is this self-same Art which is delivered unto you as an infallible doctrine. For now it hath pleased God to deliver this Doctrine again out of darkness and to fulfil his promise with thee for the Books of Enoch. And to thee he sayeth as he said to Enoch: *Let those that are worthy understand this, by thee, that it be one witness of my promise towards thee.*

## CHAPTER V

# THE NATURE OF THIS WISDOM.

§1. *To whom this Wisdom is to be Spoken.*

HIS WISDOM IS NOT TO BE SPOKEN OF IN ANY OTHER thing, neither is it to be talked of with man's imagination. For this work is the gift of God, which is all power, and so doth He open it in a tongue of power, to the intent that the proportions may agree in themselves. For it is written, Wisdom sitteth upon a hill, and beholdeth the four winds, and girdeth herself together as the brightness of the morning. But she is visited by only a few, and dwelleth alone as though she were a widow.

§2. *Concerning the Tables of Enoch.*

We instruct and inform you, according to this Doctrine delivered, that which is contained in the 49 Tables. In 49 voyces, or callings, which are the Natural Keyes to open those (not 49 but 48, for One is not to be opened) Gates of understanding. You shall have knowledge to move every Gate, and to call out as many as you please, or shall be thought necessary. They can very well, righteously, and wisely open unto you the secrets of their Cities, and make you understand perfectly that which is contained in the Tables. Through this knowledge you shall easily be able to judge, not as the world doth, but perfectly: of the world, of all things contained within the compass of Nature, and of all things which are subject to an end.

§3. *Concerning the Angelic Calls or Keys.*

Unto this Doctrine belongeth the perfect knowledge, and remembrance of the mystical Creatures. In these keys which we deliver, are the mysteries and secret beings and effects of all things moving, and moved within the world. These calls touch all parts of the World. The World may be dealt with, and her parts; therefore you may do anything. These calls are the keys into the Gates and Cities of wisdom, which cannot be opened, but with visible apparition. This is according to the former instructions and is to be had by the calling of every Table.

These are the holy and mystical Calls delivered, which followeth in practice for the moving of the Tables that control the Kings and Ministers of government. Their utterance is of force, and moveth them to visible apparition. Moved and appeared, they are forced (by the Covenant of God delivered by his spirit) to render obedient and faithful society. They will open the mysteries of their creation, as far as shall be necessary: and give you understanding of many thousand secrets, wherein you are yet but children. For every Table hath his key, every key openeth his gate, and every gate being opened, giveth knowledge of himself, of the entrance, and of the mysteries of those things whereof he is an enclosure. Within these Palaces you shall find things that are of power. For every Palace is above his City and every City above his entrance.

In these keys which we deliver, are the mysteries and secret beings and effects of all things moving, and moved within the world. In this is the life of MOTION, in whom all tongues of the world are moved, for there is neither speech nor silence that was or shall be to the end of the world.

§4. *Concerning the Primæval Language.*

Thus you see the necessity of this tongue, the excellency of it, and why it is preferred before that which you call Hebrew. For it is written that every lesser consenteth to its greater. Our wisdom shall prove Rhetoric. In this language, every letter signifieth the member of the substance whereof it speaketh. Every word signifieth the essence of the substance. The letters are separated, and in confusion: and therefore, are by numbers gathered together, which also signify a number. For as every greater containeth his lesser, so are secret and unknown forms of things knit up in their parents. Being known in number, they are easily distinguished, so that herein we teach places to be numbered, letters to be elected from the numbered, and proper words from the letters, which signify substantially the thing that is spoken of in the center of the Creator.

Even as the mind of man is moved at an ordered speech, and is easily persuaded in things that are true, so are the creatures of God stirred up in themselves when they hear the words with which they were nursed and brought forth. For nothing moveth, that is not persuaded; neither can anything be persuaded that is unknown. Without this language, the Creatures of God understand you not. You are not of their Cities; you are become enemies, because you are separated by ignorance from Him that governeth the City.

§5. *Concerning the 91 Earthly Princes.*

The Call of the Thirty Aires summons the 91 Princes and spiritual Governors unto whom the earth is delivered as a portion. They bring in and depose kings and all governments upon the earth, and they vary the natures of things with the variation of every moment. Unto them, the providence of the æternal judgement is already opened. They are governed by the 12 angels of the 12 Tribes, which are, in turn, governed by the 7 that stand before the presence of God.

Let him that can see, look up. Let him that can hear, attend, for this is wisdom. They are all spirits of the Air, not rejected, but dignified. They dwell and have their habitation in the air, in diverse and sundry places, for their mansions are not alike, nor are their powers equal. Understand, therefore, that from the fire to the earth, there are 30 places or abidings, one above and beneath another, wherein these Creatures have their abode, for a time.

§6. *Concerning the Great Table of the Quarters.*

THE GREAT TABLE OF THE QUARTERS CONTAINETH THE FOLLOWing: 1. All human knowledge. 2. Out of it springeth Physic. 3. The knowledge of all elemental Creatures amongst you, how many kinds there are, and for what use they were created, those that live in the air, those that live in the waters, those that dwell in the earth, and those of the fire (which is the secret life of all things). 4. The knowledge, finding, and use of metals, the virtues of them, the congelations and virtues of stones. 5. The conjoining and knitting together of natures. The destruction of all nature and of things that may perish. 6. Moving from place to place, as, in this country or that country at your pleasure. 7. The knowledge of all mechanical crafts. 8. The transmutation of form, but not essence. 9. The knowledge of the secrets of men.

## CHAPTER VI

# GENERAL CONSIDERATIONS OF THIS ART.

§1. *Art Thou Worthy to Read ?*

THUS saith the messengers of the God of Wisdom: Is your worthiness such that you merit such great mercy ? Are your vessels cleansed and made apt to receive and hold the sweet liquor of pure understanding ? Be not proud of the gifts of God, but become humble. Do not justify yourself in respect that this is the word of God delivered unto you for your own selves. The more you receive, be the more thankful. The more you be in the strength of God, the more use you the pureness of humility.

You called for Wisdom, and God hath opened unto you his Judgement. He hath delivered unto you the keys that you may enter. But be humble. Enter not of presumption, but of permission. Go not in rashly, but be brought in willingly. For many have ascended, but few have entered. Therefore be diligent that you may enter in, not as spoilers, but as such as deserve entertainment in the name and through the power of the Highest. For great are the mercies of God unto such as have faith.

§2. *Deal not with Wicked Spirits.*

As long as thou dealest with wicked spirits, the Lord will keep back his hands and thou keepest back the Lord. If thou wilt be the minister of God, if thou wilt go forward in His work, if thou wilt see the happy times that are to come, thou must abstain from evil. Thou must sweep thy house clean. Thou must put on thy best garments and must become humble and meek.

Let not thy life be a scandle to the will of the Lord, and to the greatness of his works. For the power that is within thy soul is of great force and the ability to perform those things that proceed with power. This is the cause that the wicked ones obey thee, for they fear themselves when they see the seal of thy Creation. Remember that there is a continual fight between us and Satan, wherein we vanquish by patience. The Devil is the father of carping, so doth he subtly infect the Seer's imagination, mingling unperfect forms with my utterance. Water is not received without air, neither the word of God without blasphemous insinuation. The son of God never did convert all, neither did all that did hear him, believe. Therefore, where the power of God is, is also Satan.

§3 .*Concerning the Book, Vestments, & Days.*

ﬤThe book consisteth first of the invocation of the names of God, and second of the invocation of the Angels, by the names of God. Their offices are manifest. ﬤFour days after your book is made, you must only call upon those names of God or of the God of Hosts, in those names. And 14 days after, you shall (in some convenient place) call the Angels by petition and by the name of God unto which they are obedient. ﬤ On the fifteenth day, you shall cloth yourselves in vestures made of white linen and so have the apparition, use, and practice of the Creatures. ﬤFor this Art is not a labour of years, nor many days.

§4. *Conclusion.*

ﬤThus hath God kept promise with you, and hath delivered you the keys to his storehouses, wherein you shall find (if you enter wisely, humbly, and patiently) treasures worth more than the frames of the heavens. Therefore, examine your books. Confer one place with another, and learn to be perfect for the practice and entrance.

ﬤThinkest thou that we speak anything that is not true ? Then thou shalt never know the mysteries of all the things that have been spoken. If you love together and dwell together, and in one God, then God will be merciful unto you, bless you, comfort you, and strengthen you unto the end. More would I say but words profit not. God be amongst you.

# BOOK TWO

# THE MYSTICAL HEPTARCHY

## OF THE DIVINE CREATION ITSELF
## TO BE READ BY THE FAITHFUL

ℳ ℳ ℳ

### CHAPTER I.

## OF THE TITLE & GENERAL CONTENTS
## OF THIS BOOK WITH SOME
## NEEDFUL TESTIMONIES

#### PRINCE BRALGES

EWARE OF WAVERING AND BLOT OUT SUSPICION, for we are God's creatures that have reigned, do reign, and shall reign forever. Behold, our mysteries shall be known unto you, preserving the secrets of Him that reigneth forever and whose name is great forever.

#### KING CARMARA

ℳOpen your eyes and you shall see from the highest to the lowest and the peace of God shall be upon you. Come, gradually we repeat the work of God. There is one God and one are his works.

#### DEE

ℳNote that this Book of Creation speaks firstly of the mighty works of God and secondly of the kings that perform these great works. Very many came upon the curved surface of the transparent globe and said: *We are prepared to serve our God.*

#### KING CARMARA

ℳThis work shall have relation to time present and present use, to mysteries far exceeding it, and finally to a purpose and intent whereby the majesty and name of God shall and may, and, of

17

B

force, must appear with the apparition of his wonders and marvels yet unheard of. So say I.

**DEE**

⚭As Michæl and Uriel at the beginning of these revealed mysteries were present and gave authority to Carmara to order the whole Heptarchical Revelation; so at the conclusion, they appeared again, and Raphæl with them; and Michæl concluded the second book of this particular revelation Heptarchical with these words following:

**MICHÆL**

⚭Merciful is our God and glorious is his name, which chooseth his creatures according to his own secret judgement. This Art is thr first part of a threefold Art joining Man with the knowledge of the world, the government of his creatures, and the sight of his majesty. This is (O I say unto you) that which is strength, medicine, and mercy to those that fear him. Amen.

**KING CARMARA**

⚭Thou hast a work of three proportions in essence, and of seven in form, which is (of itself) divided by a number sevenfold: of the course, estate, and determination of things above, things near, and things below, which of itself, is pure, perfect, and without blemish. ⚭Oh God, how easy is this first understanding ! Thou hast been told perfectly, plainly, and absolutely, not only of the condition, dignities, and estate of all things that God hath framed, but also, thou wast delivered the most perfect form and use of them. ⚭Even as God is just, His judgements true, His mercies unspeakable, so are we the true messengers of God.

**MICHÆL**

⚭Now you touch the world and the doings upon Earth. Now we show unto you the lower world and the governors that work and rule under God. By them you will have power to work such things as shall be to God's glory, and the profit of your country and the knowledge of his Creatures. They proceed from one God, one knowledge, and one operation. Come, my sons, behold these tables. Herein lie the names, that work under God upon the earth, not of the wicked, but of the Angels of light. The whole government doth consist in the hands of 49, (in God his Power, Strength, Mercy, and Justice) whose names are here evident, excellent, and glorious. Mark these tables, mark them, record them to your comfort. This is the first knowledge. Herein shall you find wisdom. Halleluiah. Mighty and Omnipotent art thou, O God, God, God, amongst thy creatures. Thou fillest all things with thy excellent foresight. Thy glory be amongst us forever. Amen.

### URIEL

⚹The fountain of wisdom is opened. Nature shall be known. The earth with her secrets shall be disclosed. The elements with their power shall be divulged.

⚹Behold, I teach! There are 49 Angels, glorious and excellent, appointed for the government of all earthly actions. These 49 do work and dispose the will of the Creator, being limited from the beginning in strength, power, and glory. These shall be subject unto you, in the name and by invocating upon the name of God, who doth lighten, dispose, and comfort you.

### KING CARMARA

⚹What doth heaven behold or the earth contain that is not or may be subdued, formed, and made by these? What learning grounded upon wisdom with the excellencies in nature cannot they manifest?

  ♄ One in Heaven they know.

  ♄ One & all in Man they know.

  ♄ One & all in Earth they know.

⚹Measure Heaven by a part (my meaning is by those few). Let God be glorified, his name praised, for his creation will be taken and his creatures well used.

Bʙ

URIEL

℥He that standeth in the midst of the globe signifieth Nature. Whereupon, in the first point, is the use and practice of this work. That is to say, concerning the first part, for it is said: The book containeth three kinds of knowledge:

℥ The knowledge of God truly.

℥ The number & doings of His Angels perfectly.

℥ The beginning & ending of Nature substantially.

# OF JOHN DEE & HIS INTEREST TO
# EXERCISE THE DOCTRINE HEPTARCHICAL

### URIEL

HIS, YOUR ERA, IS THE LAST AGE, WHICH WILL BE revealed unto you. The mysteries of God have a time. The Sons of Light and their Sons are subject unto my commandment. This is a mystery. I have spoken of it; note it thoroughly. They are my servants. By them thou shalt work marvels.

### PRINCE HAGONEL

⚜There are kings false and unjust, whose power I have subverted and destroyed. So shalt thou.

⚜The second assembly were the governors of the Earth, whose glory (if they be good) the weapons we have taught thee will augment, and, consequently (if they be evil) will perverr.

### PRINCE BORNOGO

⚜I am Bornogo. What thou desirest shall be fulfilled. Glory to God.

### PRINCE BEFAFES

⚜Behold, Behold, Lo Behold, my mighty power consisteth in this. Learn wisdom by my words. This is wrought for thy erudition, what I instruct thee from God. Look to thy charge truly. Thou art yet dead. Thou shalt be revived. But Oh, bless God truly. The blessing that God giveth me I will bestow upon thee by permission. O how mighty is our God, which walked on the waters, which sealed me with His name, whose glory is without end. Thou hast written me, but yet dost not know me. Use me,

in the Name of God; I shall, at the time appointed, be ready. I
will manifest the works  of the seas and the miracles of the deep
shall be known.

### KING CARMARA

Behold, thou desirest and art sick with desire. I am the disposer
though not the composer of God's medicines. Thou desirest to
be comforted and strengthened in thy labours. I minister unto
thee the Strength of God. What I say is not of myself. Neither
that which is said to me, is of themselves; but is said of Him which
liveth forever. These mysteries hath God lastly, and of His great
mercies granted unto thee. I have answered thy doubting mind.
Thou shalt be glutted, yea filled, yea thou shalt swell and be puffed
up with the perfect knowledge of God's mysteries in His mercies.
Abuse them not. Be faithful; use mercy. God shall enrich thee.
Banish Wrath—It was the first and the greatest commandment.
I reign by Him and live by Him which reigneth  and  liveth
forever.

I have showed thee perfectly. Behold I teach again. O how
merciful is God, that revealeth such great secrets to flesh and blood!
Thou has 42 letters. Thy tables last, contain so many.

When thou wilt work for anything pertaining to the estate of
a good king, thou must first call upon him which is their prince.
Secondly, the ministers of his power are six.

In outward sense  my words are true. I speak now of the use
of one of the first that I speak of, or manifested yesterday. Said
I not and showed I not the Government of princes, for as
it is a mystery to a further matter,  so it is a purpose to a
present use. If it rules worldly princes, how much more shall it
work with the Princes of Creation ? Thou desirest use; I teach
thee use. And yet the Art is to the further understanding of all
sciences that are past, present, and yet to come. Fruits hath further virtue, but only in the eating. Gold has further condition,
property and quality, than in melting or in common use. Kings

there are in Nature, with Nature, and above Nature. Thou art dignified in this knowledge.

Last of all, thy ring, which was appointed thee, with the lamen comprehending the form of thy own name, which is to be made in perfect gold, as is aforesaid.

Thou shalt be comforted. But respect the world, whereunto thou art provided; and for what end; and that in what time. Serve God truly; serve Him justly. Great care is to be had with those that meddle with Prince's affairs. Much more consideration with whom thou shalt meddle or use any practice. But God hath shadowed thee from destruction. He preserveth His faithful, and shaddoweth the just with a shield of honour. None shall enter into the knowledge of these mysteries with thee, but this worker*. Thy estate with the Prince (now reigning)† shall shortly be amended, her favour increased, with the good will of diverse that are now deceivers. Thy hand shall shortly be their help; and thou shalt do wonderful and many benefits (to the augmenting of God's Glory) for thy country. Finally, God doth enrich thee with knowledge and of thyself hath given thee understanding of these worldly vanities. He is merciful and his good creatures neither have, do, nor will forget thee. God bless you both; whose Mercy, Goodness, and Grace I pronounce and utter upon you.

### KING BOBOGEL

I have said: *Dee, Dee, Dee* at length, but not too late‡.

### KING CARMARA

Lo, thus thou seest the glory of God's creatures; whom thou mayest use with the consideration of the day, their King, their Prince and his Character. The King and Prince govern for the whole day; the rest according to the sixth part of the day. Use

---

* *i. e.* Kelly
† *i. e.* Queen Elizabeth
‡ Dee's note: King Bobogel said this of my attaining to such mysteries as the ministers under him made show of.

them to the glory, praise, and honour of Him which created them, to the laude and praise of His Majesty.

### KING BYNEPOR

ঙWrite this reverently. Note it with submission. What I speak hath not been revealed; no not in the last times of the second last world. Thou shalt work marvels marvelously by my workmanship in the highest.

### KING BNASPOL

ঙUnto my Prince (my subject) are delivered the keys of the mysteries of the Earth. All those are Angels that govern under him. Use them; they are and shall be at thy commandment.

### KING BNASPEN

ঙBy me thou shalt cast out the power of wicked spirits. By me thou shalt know the doings and practices of evil men, and more than may be spoken or uttered to man.

### KING CARMARA

ঙOh, how great is the sickness and corruption of man who barely has faith in God or in His good Angels? You maketh all the earthly things that have the corruption of the earth within them. Our God, our God, He is our God. It is true we are His Angels and it is also true that we are His servants. I ask for that power. I speak, and that which I speak is the shadow of truth, justice, and perfection.

   ঙ BEHOLD: (Holding up the measuring rod.)
   ঙ HERE: (Pointing to the end of the rod.)
   ঙ AND HERE: (Pointing to the middle of it.)

ঙI bear a power and virtue that is beyond measure. Nothing is obscure which is received through him. ঙOne thing is yet wanting; a meet receptacle. There is yet wanting a stone. One there is most excellent; hid in the secret part of the depths in the uttermost part of the Roman possession. Lo, the right hand of God is upon thee. Thou shalt prevail with it, with Kings and with all Creatures of the world; whose beauty (in virtue) shall be more worth than the Kingdoms of the Earth. Go towards it and take it up. Keep it secret. Let no mortal hand touch it but thine own.

## IL

⚹Thy character must have the names of the six angels (written in the midst of the Sigillum Æmeth) graven upon the other side in a circle, in the midst where must the stone be (which was also brought). Wherein thou shalt at all times behold (privately to thyself) the state of God's people, through the whole world.

### RAPHÆL

⚹Go and thou shalt receive. Tarry and thou shalt receive. Sleep and thou shalt see. But watch, and thine eyes shall be fully opened. One thing which is the ground and element of thy desire is already perfected. Out of seven thou hast been instructed (of the lesser part) most perfectly. ⚹All those before spoken of are subject to thy call. Of friendship at any time thou mayest see them and know what thou wilt. Every one (to be short) shall at all times and seasons, show thee direction in anything.⚹One thing, I answer thee for all offices. Thou hast in subjection all offices. Use them when it pleaseth thee and as thy instruction hath been.

### URIEL

⚹The Lord saith: *I have hardened the heart of one of you. Yea, I have hardened him , as the flint, and burnt him together with the ashes of a cedar, to the intent he may be proved just in my work, and great the strength of my glory. Neither shall his mind consent to the wickedness of iniquity, for from iniquity I have chosen him to be a first earthly witness of my dignity.* *

### DEE

⚹Uriel came in again and another with him and jointly they did say together: *Glorify God forever.* And now Uriel stood behind and the other sat down in the chair with a sword in his right hand. All his head glittered like the sun; the hair of his head was

* Apparently Uriel is refering to Kelly.

long. He had wings and all his lower parts seemed to be with feathers. He had a robe over his body and a great light in his left hand. He said: *We are blessed from the beginning and blessed be the name of God forever†.*

⚹An innumerable company of angels were about him. And Uriel didst lean on the square table. Then he that sat on the chair said to them:

*Go forward, God hath blessed thee.*
*I will be thy Guide.*
*Thou shalt attain unto thy Searching,*
*The world begins with thy doings.*
    *Praise God.*
*The Angels under my power shall be*
*at thy commandment.*
*Thou shalt see me.*
*I will be seen of thee.*
*I will direct thy Living & Conversation.*

⚹Now Michæl thrust out his right Arm with the sword. I bade the Skryer to look. Then the sword did seem to cleave in two. And a great fire flamed out of it vehemently. Then he took a ring out of the flames of his sword and gave it to Uriel and said: *The Strength of God is unspeakable. Praise be to God for ever & ever.* And Uriel did make curtsy to him. Then Michæl did say the following:

### MICHÆL

⚹After this sort must be the ring. Note it. I will reveal thee this ring, which was never revealed since the death of Solomon, with whom I was present. I was present with him in strength and mercy. Lo, this it is. This it is wherewith all miracles and divine works and wonders were wrought by Solomon. This it is which I have revealed unto thee. This it is which Philosophie dreameth of. This it is which the Angels scarce know. This it

† Dee's note: This was Michæl and his manner of apparition.

is and blessed by his name, yea his name be blessed forever. There
are kings false and unjust, whose power thou mayest subvert &
destroy.

DEE

⚡Then he laid the ring down upon the Table and said: Note. I
noted the manner of the ring in all points. After that he threw
the ring down upon the table and it seemed to fall through the
table. And then he said the following:

MICHÆL

⚡So shall it do at thy commandments. Without this ring thou
shalt do nothing. Blessed be his Name that compasseth all things.
Wonders are in him and his Name is wonderful. His Name work-
eth wonders from generation to generation.

DEE

⚡Then Michæl brought in the seal which he showed the other
day and opened his sword and had the Skryer read. And he read
ÆMETH. Then the sword closed up again and Michæl said the
following:

MICHÆL

⚡This I do open unto thee because thou marvelest at the Sigil of
God. This is the name of the Seal which be blessed forever. This
is the seal itself. This is holy. This is pure. This is forever. Amen.
⚡As truely as I was with Solomon, so truely will I be with thee.
I was with Solomon in all his works and wonders. Use me, in
the Name of God, for all occasions.

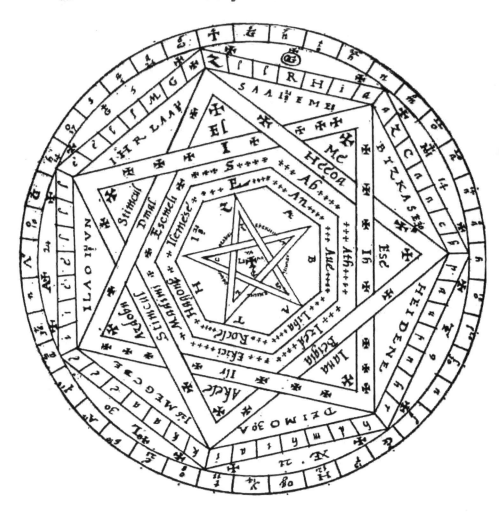

THE SIGIL OF ÆMETH

# SOME REMEMBRANCES OF THE FURNITURE & CIRCUMSTANCES NECESSARY IN THE EXERCISE HEPTARCHICAL

## KING CARMARA

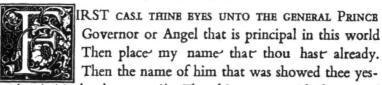IRST CAST THINE EYES UNTO THE GENERAL PRINCE Governor or Angel that is principal in this world Then place my name that thou hast already. Then the name of him that was showed thee yesterday (with the short coat*). Then his power, with the rest of his six perfect ministers. With these three thou shalt work to a good end. All the rest thou may use to God's glory for every one of them shall minister to thy necessities. ✠Moreover, when thou invokest, thy feet must be placed upon these tables which thou seest written last, comprehending 42 letters and names. But with this consideration: that the character (which is the first of the 7 in the former book) be placed upon the top of the table, which thou wast and art and shall be commanded to have and use. ✠Last of all the ring which was appointed thee, with the lamen comprehending the form of thy own name; which is to be made in perfect gold as is aforesaid.

✠Even as God is just, his judgements true, his mercies unspeakable; so are we the true messengers of God and our words are true in His mercy forever. Glory, Oh Glory be to thou, Oh most high God. ✠Lo, thus thou seest the Glory of God's creatures; whom thou mayest use with the consideration of the day, their

* Prince Hagonel

King, their Prince, and his character. The King and Prince govern for the whole day; the rest according to the six parts of the day. Use them to the glory, praise, and honour of Him, which created them, to the laude and praise of His majesty. The characters of the Kings are in the Globe; and the characters of the Princes are in the Heptagon.

### PRINCE HAGONEL

꙰The Sons of Light snd their Sons are subject to my commandment. This is a mystery. I have spoken of it. Note it thoroughly. They are my servants. By them thou shalt work marvels. My time᾽ is yet to come᾽. The operations of the earth are subject to my power. I am the first of twelve. My seal is called 'Barces' & here it is. In his name with my name by my character and the rest of my ministers are these things brought to pass.

꙰These that lie here are Witches, Enchanters, Deceivers, and Blasphemers. And finally all they that offer Nature with abuse and dishonour Him which reigneth forever. ꙰The second assembly were the governors of the earth, whose glory, if they be good, the weapons which we have brought thee will augment, and consequently (if they be evil) will pervert. ꙰The third assembly are those which taste of God's mysteries and drink of the juice of Nature, and whose minds are divided, some with eyes looking towards heaven, the rest to the center of the earth. Where God's glory is not, there neither are the good, nor goodness.

꙰It is wrought (I say) it is wrought (for thy understanding) by the seven of the seven, which were the sons of æternity, whose names thou hast written and recorded to God's glory.

### PRINCE BUTMONO

꙰Mark this*: All spirits inhabiting within the earth where their habitation is of force, not of will, are subject to the power here

---

* Dee's note: Prince Butmono said this, but the office is under King Bnaspol, whose Prince is Blisdon. The mystery of this I know not yet, for Blisdon will be found to be the proper minister of King Bnaspol.

within my seal: with this you shall govern; with this you shall unlock; with this (in his Name who reigneth) you shall discover the entrance.

### KING CARMARA

⚮Secondly, the ministers of his power are six, whose names contain seven letters apiece. So thy tables do manifest. By whom in generality, or by any one of them in particularity, thou shalt work for any intent or purpose. As concerning the letters particularly, they do concern the names of 42, which 42 in generally, or one of them, do and can work the destruction, hinderance, or annoyance of the estate, condition, or degree (as well for a body of government) of any wicked or ill-living prince.

⚮*Venito Bobogel, Rex et Princeps Nobilitatis; Venito cum Ministris; Venito (inquam) venito cum Satellitibus tuis, minutus†.*

[Come Bobogel, Noble Prince & King. Come with your ministers. Come, yea, come with your satellites.]

### KING BOBOGEL

⚮*Veni Princepes & Principum, qui sunt Aquarum Principes; Ego sum Rex Potens et mirabilis in Aquis; cuius potestas est aquarum viceribus.‡*

[Come, O thou who are Princes of the waters. I am the King, powerful and wonderous in the waters, whose power is over the waters.]

### KING CARMARA

⚮*Venito veni (inquam) Adesto. Veni Rex. O Rex, Rex, Rex Aquarum. Venito, Venito, (inquam). Magna est tua. Major autem mea potestas. Vitam dedit Deum omnibus creaturis.*

[Come, I say, come at this time. Come, O King, King, King of the waters. Your power is great but my power is greater. God gave life to all creatures.]

### KING CARMARA

⚮*Veni Ignis, Veni vita mortalium (inquam) ventio. Adesdum. Regnat Deus, O Venite. Nam unus illo. Regnat, et est vita viventium.*

† Dee's note: This I note for the form of calling.
‡ Dee's note: This is King Bobogel's call to his Prince.

[Come, O fire, which is the life of all mortal things. Come at this time. God Reigns. O come, for he is one. He reigns and is the life of all living things.]

#### KING CARMARA

*Venite, ubi nulla quius sed stridor dentium. Venite vos, qui sub meæ estis potestate.*

[Come, where there is nothing of him but the gnashing of teeth. Come, all of you who are under my power.]

Behold, every one of these princes must have his peculiar table.

#### URIEL

Thy character must have the names of the seven Angels (written in the midst of the Sigil of Æmeth) graven upon the other side in a circle. In the midst whereof must the stone be, which was also brought, wherein thou shalt at all times behold (private to thyself) the state of God's people through the whole earth.

The four feet of the table must have 4 hollow things of sweet wood, whereupon they must stand. Within the hollow spheres thy seals may be kept unperished. One month is all for the use thereof. The silks must be of diverse colours, the most changeable that can be gotten, for who is able to behold the Glory of the Seat of God ?

#### DEE

The character or lamen for me was noted that it should contain some token of my name. And now in this accounted the true character of dignification, I perceive no peculiar mark or letters of my name.

#### URIEL

The form in every corner considereth your name.

#### DEE

You mean there to be a certain shadow of Delta‡?

#### URIEL

Well.

‡ Dee used a delta (triangle) to represent his name.

**DEE**

What is the use of these tables? From what ground are they framed or divided?

**URIEL**

They are the ensignias of the creation wherewith all they were created by God: known only by their acquaintance and the manner of their doings.

**DEE**

Have I rightly applied the days to the Kings?

**URIEL**

The days are rightly applied to the Kings.

**DEE**

The characters and words, annexed to the Kings' names in the outer circumference of the great circle or globe: how are they to be used?

**URIEL**

They are to be painted on sweet wood and so to be held in thy hand as thou shalt have cause to use them.

**IL\***

The Sigil of Æmeth is to be set in the middle of the table. Grace, Mercy, and Peace be unto the lively branches of his flourishing kingdoms. And strong art thou in their glory which dost unknit the secret part of thy lively workmanship; and that before the weak understanding of men. Herein is thy power and magnificence opened unto Man. And why? Because thy divinity and secret power is here shut up in the third and fourth number; from the first and fundamental is of all your most holy works. For if thou (O God) be wonderful and incomprehensible in thine own substance, it must needs follow that thy works are likewise incomprehensible. But lo, they shall now believe, because they see that which heretofore they could scarcely believe. Strong is

* Dee's note: IL is the first of the seven Sons of Light. IL is the always adherent minister to King Baligon and his name is expressed in his character.

C

the influence of thy supercelestial power, and mighty is the force of thy arm which overcometh all things. Let all power therefore rest in thee. Amen.

⚜Leave out the letter 'B' of the seven names of the Kings and seven princes and place them in a table divided by 12 and 7, the seven spaces being uppermost. And therein write in the upper line, the letters of the King, with the letters of his prince following just after his name. And so of the six others and their princes. And read them on the right hand, from the upper part to the lowest. And thou shalt find, then, the composition of this table. ⚜Therein they are all comprehended, saving certain letters which are not to be put in here. By reason that the Kings and Princes do spring from God, and not God from the Kings and Princes. Which excellency is comprehended and is also manifest in that third and fourth number round about the sides (of this square table) is every letter of the 14 names of the seven kings and princes. ⚜Hereafter shall you perceive that the glory of this table surmounteth the glory of the sun. All things also that appertain unto it are already proscribed by your former instruction.

⚜God is the beginning of all things, but not after one sort, nor to every one alike. But there are three manners of working with His name: ☽ 1: in respect of dignification; ☽ 2: in respect of conciliation; ☽ 3: in respect to the end & determined operation. ⚜Now as to what and would you wear your characters, &c. But how do I teach ? The character is an instrument applicable only to dignification. But there is no dignification but that which doth proceed and hath his perfect composition centrally in the square number of 3 & 4, the center whereof and shall be equal to the greatest. Hereby you may gather not only to what end, the blessed character (wherewith thou shalt be dignified) is prepared, but also the name of all other characters.

⚜The table is the instrument of conciliation, and so are proper to every King and Prince, according to their order.

⚬Now as to the last, concerning the end and determination. It only consisteth in the mercy of God and the characters of these books. Set down the Kings and their Princes in a table, as thou knowest them, with their letters backward (excepting their "B's") from the right hand to the left. Let Bobogel be the first and Bornogo his prince, &c.‡

### DEE

⚬So on my character or lamen of dignification are all the names of the seven kings and all the seven princes, perfect as in the great table, the "B's" only being the first letter common to them all, kept back, but in memory.

### MICHÆL

⚬I will now speak concerning the Sigil of Æmeth, called also the Sigil of God. I will show thee in the mighty hand and strength of God, what His mysteries are, the true circle of Æternity, comprehending all virtue, the whole and sacred trinity. Oh holy be he; Oh holy be he; Oh holy be he. Amen. ⚬Now what wilt thou?

### DEE

⚬I would full fain proceed according to the matter in hand.

### MICHÆL

⚬Divide this outward circle into 40 equal parts, whose greatest numbers are four. See that thou do it presently.

### DEE

⚬I did so dividing it first into four parts and then every one of them by ten. ⚬Michæl then called out by name *Semiel*. One came in and knelt down and great fire came out of his mouth.

### MICHÆL

⚬To this one named Semiel, are the mysteries of this table known. ⚬Oh God, thou hast said and thou livest forever.

‡ Dee's note: It may appear that Butmono is Prince to Bynepor and Blisdon Prince to King Bnaspol.

Cc

DEE

Semiel then stood up, and flaming fire came out of his mouth
and then he said as followeth: *Mighty lord: what wouldst thou
with the tables ?*

MICHÆL

It is the will of God that thou fetch them hither.

SEMIEL

I am his tables. Behold, these are his tables. Lo, where they are.

DEE

There came in 40 white creatures, all in white silk long robes,
and they were like children. And all of them, falling on their
knees, said: *Thou only art holy among the highest: Oh God, thy
Name be blessed forever.*

Michæl then stood up out of his chair and, by & by, all his legs
seemed to be like two pillars of brass, and he was as high as half-
way up to heaven. And, by and by, his sword was all on fire.
And he shook and drew his sword over the heads of all these 40
and they fell down. Then Michæl spake to Semiel with a thundering voice:

MICHÆL

Declare the mysteries of the Living God; our God; of One
that liveth forever !

SEMIEL

I am ready.

DEE

Michael shook over them with his sword and they all fell down
(and Uriel also) on their knees. And commonly at the striking
with the sword, flaming fire like lightning, did flash.

MICHÆL

Note: Here is a mystery.

DEE

Then stept forth one of the 40 from the rest and opened his
breast, which was covered with silk, and there appeared on it a

great 'T' all of gold. And over the 'T' stood the number '4'. The 40 all cried: *It liveth and multiplieth forever; blessed be his Name.* Then that creature did shut up his bosom and vanished away like fire.

### MICHÆL

⚜Place that in the first place. It is the name of God.

### DEE

⚜Then there seemed a great clap of Thunder\*. . . The chair was brought in again and I asked what it meant.

### URIEL

⚜This is a seat of perfection, from which things shall be showed unto thee, which thou hast long desired.

### DEE

⚜Then was a square table brought into the stone and I demanded what that table betokened.

### URIEL

⚜A mystery not yet to be known. These two shall remain in the same stone to the sight of all undefiled creatures. ⚜You must use a four-square table, two cubits square, whereupon must be set the Sigil of God. This seal is not to be looked upon without great reverence and devotion. This seal is to be made of perfect wax. The seal must be 9 inches in diameter. The roundness must be 27 inches or somewhat more. The thickness of it must be an inch and a half to an inch and a quarter. And a figure of a cross must be on the backside of it made thus:

---

\* Dee's note: And so forth. And note that the whole second book is nothing else but the Mysteries most marvelous of the Sigil of God, sometimes called the Sigil of Æmeth, wherein here I did leave but a little exerpt. Note further that almost all the third book was of the seven ensignias of creation whereof mention was before made.

The table is to be made of sweet wood and of two cubits high, with four feet with four of the former seals under the four feet.
Under the table did seem to be laid red silks two yards square. And over the seal did seem likewise red silk to lie four square, broader than the table, hanging down with four tassles at the four corners thereof. Upon this uppermost red silk did seem the stone with the frame to be set, right over and upon the principal seals, saving that the red silk was between the one and the other.
There appeared the first table covered with a cloth of silk of changeable colour, red and green, with a white cloth under it hanging very low.

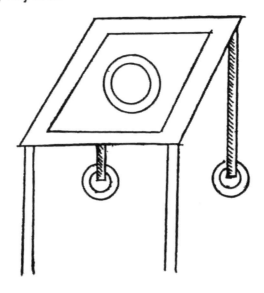

## CHAPTER IV

# SOME NOTICE OF THE PECULIAR FORMS & ATTIRE
## WHERE-IN THE KINGS, PRINCES
## & MINISTERS HEPTARCHICAL APPEARED
## & SOME OF THEIR ACTIONS
## & GESTURES AT THEIR APPEARANCE

### KING CARMARA

HIS KING (BEING CALLED FIRST BY URIEL) APPEARED as a man, very well proportioned and clad in a long purple robe with a triple crown of gold upon his head.

At his first coming he had seven spirits (like men) waiting on him, which afterwards declared themselves to be the seven Princes Heptarchical.

Uriel delivered unto this King (at his first appearing) a rod, or straight little round staff of gold, divided into three equal distinctions, whereof two were dark or black and the third bright red. This rod he kept still in his hand.

This king only was the orderer or disposer of all the doctrine, which I term Heptarchical, and the first practitioner thereof, calling the seven Princes and after that the seven Kings, and and by giving instruction for use and practice of the whole doctrine Heptarchical. For the first purpose and fruit to be enjoyed by me, of the two other, there was only mention made.

King CARMARA said: *This is the sign of the work* and there appeared the letters 'C' and 'B' reversed on a white flag with a woman standing by, whose arms did not appear. On the other side of the flag appeared the coat of arms of England as on the old flag:

**PRINCE HAGONEL**

Note that all the Princes seemed to be men, and to have red robes, but this Prince had a robe that was shorter than the others. All the princes had circlets of gold on their heads rather than crowns or coronets. This Prince held in the palm of his right hand a round ring with a point or prick in the midst, hanging also over his middle fingers, which he affirmed to be his seal and said that the name of it was Barces:

All the princes held up together a seven-pointed star that seemed to be of copper:

THE SUBJECTS AND SERVANTS TO PRINCE HAGONEL

The Sons of Light and their Sons are said to be subject unto the commandment of HAGONEL and are his servants. Their names are all given in the sigil of Æmeth:

*The Seven Sons of Light:*

1. I
2. IH
3. ISR
4. DMAL

5. HECOA
6. BEIGIA
7. STIMCUL

*The Seven Sons of the Sons:*

1. E or IL
2. AN
3. AVE
4. LIBA
5. ROCLE
6. HAGONEL
7. ILEMESE

### THE SONS OF LIGHT

֍The seven Sons of Light appeared like seven young men, all with bright countenance, apparelled in white, with white silk on their heads. Every one seemed to have a metalic ball in his hand, the first of gold, the second of silver, the third of copper, the fourth of tin, the fifth of iron, the sixth tossed between his two hands a round thing of quicksilver, the last had a ball of lead. The first had on his breast a round tablet of gold and on it written a great 'I'. And the second, on his golden tablet, had his name also written. And every one orderly coming forth, showed their names upon their golden tablets. At their departing they made curtsy and mounted up to Heaven.

### THE SONS OF THE SONS OF LIGHT

֍The Sons of the Sons of Light appeared like seven little children, like boys covered all with purple, with hanging sleeves, like the sleeves on priests' or scholars' gowns. Their heads were attired all after the former manner with purple silk. They had three-cornered tablets on their breasts, and these tablets seemed to be very green and on them the letters of their names were written. The first had two letters made thus of an 'E' and an 'L' or 'E-'. They made reverences to Michæl (who had called them) and so mounted up to heavenwards.

### THE 42 MINISTERS OF PRINCE HAGONEL

ֈAt the call of King CARMARA (during the second handling of this Heptarchical doctrine), when he said *Come, repeat the works of God,* there appeared Prince HAGONEL, and after that followed 42, who said *We are prepared to serve our God.* Each of these had somewhat in their hands as they stood in this order, and Hagonel seemed to embrace the company:

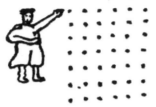

.SSix of these seemed more glorious than the rest and their coats were longer; they had circlets of gold around their heads and held in their hands perfect crowns of gold. The second six had three quarters of crowns in their hands. The third six had robes or clothes in their hands. All the rest seemed to have balls of gold, which they tossed from one to another, but at the catching they seemed empty windballs, for they grasped them by closing their hands, as if they were not solid but empty like a blown bladder. The first six made curtsy to Prince HAGONEL, the second six made curtsy to the first, and the third to the second. And they all, with Prince HAGONEL, made curtsy to King CARMARA.

.SEach of the 42 stood upon a table, and upon every table was but a single letter. The first minister of the first six did go away and in his table appeared the letter 'O' and so of the rest. But the third six cowered down and was loath to show their tables, but at length did. The third row went off, lamenting, being commanded by the Prince. All departed in fire, falling into the globe. The fifth row, too, did sink into the Globe, every one in a sundry fire by himself. The sixth row fell with smoke down into the globe. Thus was revealed the following table:

```
O E S N G L E
A V Z N I L N
Y L L M A F S
N R S O G O O
N R R C P R N
L A B D G R E
```

.S²King CARMARA said: Remember how they stood when they were secondly disposed unto thee. They stood first in six rows, and next they were turned into seven. I speak of the greater number and not of the lesser, for in speaking of the greater I have comprehended the lesser*.

---

* Dee's note: There are but 6 names that are in subjection to the Prince. The first seven next him are these which held the fair and beautiful crowns. The first seven are called by those names that thou seest: OES . . . &c.

This diversity of reckoning by 6 and 7, I cannot yet reconcile.

### THE SEAL OF AVE*

#### KING BOBOGEL

He appeared in a black velvet coat; and his hose was close round hose with velvet upperstocks, overlayed with gold lace. On his head was a velvet hat or cap with a black feather in it. A cape was hanging on one of his shoulders, and his purse was hanging about his neck. Hung upon his girdle was a rapier. His beard was long. and he had bloomers and slippers. And he said, *I wear these robes not in respect of myself, but of my Government.*†

#### PRINCE BONORGO

He appeared in a red robe with a gold circlet on his head; he shewed his seal and said : *This it is.*

#### THE 42 MINISTERS

Seven of the ministers are apparelled like BOBOGEL the king; sagely and gravely; all the rest are almost ruffian or boisterous. Some are like to be men and women; for in the forepart they seemed women, and in the back part men, by their apparel. And they were the last 7. They danced, leapt, and kissed. They came afterwards into a circle, the sage and the rest; but the sages

* A seal for each of the Sons of the Sons of Light appears at the top margin of each page where the description of each set of King, Prince and 42 Ministers begins.

† The above described robes would have been considered extremely rich and elegant in Dee's time.

stood all together. The first of the sages lifted up his hand aloft and said: *Let us follow the Will of God; Our God is truly Noble and Eternal.* He plucked up his right foot and under it appeared an 'L'. And the rest in like manner appeared their letters or names.

1. The first seven grew all together in a flame of fire and so sunk down into the transparent fiery globe of the new world.
2. The second seven fell down like dross of Metal.
3. The third seven clasped together and fell down in a thick smoke.
4. The fourth seven joined together and vanished like drops of water.
5. The fifth seven fell down like a storm of hail.
6. The last vanished away.

S₤At another time , they came (being called by King CARMARA) all 42 bringing a round table over their heads flat-wise; and they laid it down and stood about it the letters being as before.

L E E N A R B
L N A N A E B
R O E M N A B
L E A O R I B
N E I C I A B
A O I D I A B

THE SEAL OF LIBA

### KING BABALEL

He appeared with a crown of gold on his head; with a long robe whitish of colour; his left arm's sleeve was very white; and his right arm sleeve was black. He seemed to stand upon water. His name was written on his forehead: BABALEL.

### PRINCE BEFAFES

Prince Befafes appeared in a long red robe, with a circlet of gold on his head. He had a golden girdle, and on it was written BEFAFES. He opened his bosom and appeared lean; and seemed to have feathers under his robes. His seal or character was thus:

### THE 42 MINISTERS

Of his 42 ministers, the first seven had circlets of gold on their heads, and the King BABALEL called Befafes saying: *Come Prince of the Seven Princes, who are Princes over the waters.* Every one of the 42 had a letter on his forehead. They were seven in a row; and six downward. But of the first seven, the letters became to be between their feete; and the water seemeth continually to pass over these letters. The first seven took the water and threw it upwards and it became clouds. The second threw it upwards and it became snow, &c. The 42 dived into the water and so vanished away. And BABALEL and Befafes also were suddenly gone. Their names and characters appeared to be these, which follow in the squares.

```
E  I  L  O  M  F  O
N  E  O  T  P  T  A
S  A  G  A  C  I  Y
O  N  E  D  P  O  N
N  O  O  N  M  A  N
E  T  E  V  L  G  L
```

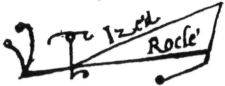

THE SEAL OF ROCLE

### KING BYNEPOR

⚜King Bynepor appeared as a King, with his Prince next after him; and after the prince, 42 ministers.

### PRINCE BUTMONO

⚜Prince Butmono appeared in a red robe, with a golden circle on his head. His seal is this:

### THE 42 MINISTERS

⚜They appeared like Ghosts and Smokes without all form, having every one of them a little glittering spark of fire in the midst of them. The first seven are red as blood. The second seven are not so red. The third seven are like whitish smoke. These three sevens had the sparks greater than the rest. The fourth, fifth, and sixth seven are of diverse colors. All had a fiery spark in their middle. Every spark had a letter in it as followeth:

```
B B A R N F L
B B A I G A O
B B A L P A E
B B A N I F G
B B O S N I A
B B A S N O D
```

THE SEAL OF AN

### KING BNASPOL

⚡King BNASPOL appeared in a red robe, and a crown on his head. His prince followed him and after him his ministers.

### PRINCE BLISDON

⚡Prince Blisdon appeared in a robe of many colours and on his head a circlet of gold.* This is his character or seal:

### THE 42 MINISTERS

⚡The 42 seemed to stand about in a little hill round. The hill was of clay. Behind this company seemed to stand an innumerable multitude of ugly people, afar off. Those which stood afar off are spirits of perdition, which keep the earth with her treasures for him, &c. These which seem to stand about the little hill seemed to have in the palms of their hands, letters in order, as here followeth:

E L G N S E B
N L I N Z V B
S F A M L L B
O O G O S R S
N R P C R R B
e r g d b a b

---

*Dee: Perhaps the red colour was most, and so seemed generally to be red as the other their robes were.

D

THE SEAL OF HAGONEL

### KING BNAPSEN

ℑℌKing Bnaspsen appeared as a king with a crown on his head.

### PRINCE BRORGES

ℑℌPrince Brorges appeared in his red apparel; and he opened his clothes and there did four mighty and most terrible and ghastly flames of fire out of his sides; which no mortal eye could abide to look upon any long while. And in marvelous raging fire the word 'Brorges' did appear tossed to and fro of the mighty flames. His seal or character is this:

### THE 42 MINISTERS

ℑℌThe 42 appeared holding a round table. They toss it in fiery flames. In the table were the letters of their names as followeth:

B A N S S Z E
B Y A P A R E
B N A M G E N
B N V A G E S
B L B O P O O
B A B E P E N

### THE SEAL OF EL

#### KING BALIGON

King BALIGON is the same mighty king who is here first described by the name of CARMARA, and yet otherwise among the Angels called MARMARA. But the 'M' is not to be expressed. Therefore he appeared in a long purple gown and on his head a triple crown of gold, with a measuring rod of gold in his hand, divided into three equal parts; in the form of a well proportioned man.

#### PRINCE BAGANOL

He appeared not by that name yet.†

#### THE 42 MINISTERS

Note that the king himself is governor over these. The 42 ministers appeared like bright people. And besides them all the air swarmed with creatures. Their letters were on their foreheads. They stood in a circle. They took their letter from their foreheads and set them in a circle.

A O A Y N N A
L B B N A A U
I O A E S P M
G G L P P S A
O E E O O E Z
N L L R L N A

† Probably Prince Hagonel under a pseudonym similar to Baligon (a.k.a. Carmara).

Dd

### THE SEAL OF ILEMESE

#### KING BLUMAZA

⚜He appeared not yet by that name.

#### PRINCE BRALGES

⚜Prince Bralges appeared in a red robe with a circlet on his head. And he was the last of the seven which hold the Heptagonon, all the rest being set down; who seemed now to extend their hands towards another, as though they played, being now rid of their work. This is the seal of his government:

#### THE 42 MINISTERS

⚜The powers under his subjection are invisible. They appeared like little white smokes without any form. All the world seemed to be in brightness.

O E S N G L E
A V Z N I L N
Y L L M A F S
N R S O G O O
N R R C P R N
L A B D G R E

## CHAPTER V

## THE ORATION TO GOD
## TO BE SPOKEN EVERY DAY,
## THREE TIMES SUCCESSIVELY

ALMIGHTY, ÆTERNAL, THE TRUE AND LIVING GOD: O King of Glory, O Lord of Hosts, O Thou, the Creator of Heaven and Earth, and of all things visible and invisible: Now, (even now, at length,) among other Thy manifold mercies used, and to be used toward me, Thy simple servant, JOHN DEE, I most humbly beseech Thee, in this my present petition to have mercy upon me, to have pity upon me, to have compassion upon me. I, faithfully and sincerely, of long time, have sought among men, in Earth, and also by prayer (full oft and pitifully) have made suit unto Thy Divine Majesty for the obtaining of some convenient portion of True Knowledge and Understanding of Thy laws and ordinances, established in the natures and properties of Thy Creatures: By which Knowledge, Thy Divine Wisdom, Power and Goodness, (on Thy Creatures bestowed and to them imparted), being to me made and allure me, (for the same) incessantly to pronounce Thy praises, to render unto Thee, most hearty thanks, to advance Thy true honour, and to win unto Thy Name, some of Thy due Majestic Glory, among all people, and forever. And, whereas, it hath pleased Thee (O God) of Thy infinite Goodness, by Thy faithful and holy Spiritual Messengers, to deliver unto me, long since (through the eye and ear of E. K.) an orderly form, and manner of exercise Heptarchical: How, (to Thy Honour and Glory, and the Comfort of my own poor soul, and of others, Thy faithful servants,) I may, at all times, use very many of Thy

good Angels, their counsels and helps; according to the properties of such their functions, and offices, as to them, by Thy Divine Power, Wisdom and Goodness, is assigned, and limited:
(Which orderly form, and manner of exercise, until even now, I
never found opportunity and extreme necessity, to apply myself
unto,) Therefore, I thy poor, and simple servant, do most humbly, heartily, and faithfully beseech Thy Divine Majesty, most
lovingly and fatherly to favour: and by Thy Divine Beck to
further this my present industry and endeavour to exercise myself,
according to the foresaid orderly forme and manner: And, now,
(at length, but not too late) for Thy dearly beloved Son IESUS
CHRIST His sake, (O Heavenly Father) to grant also unto me,
this blessing and portion of Thy heavenly Graces: That Thou
wilt forthwith, enable me, make me apt and acceptable, (in body,
soul, and spirit) to enjoy always the holy and friendly conversation, with the sensible, plain, full, and perfect help, in word and
deed , of Thy Mighty, Wise, and Good Spiritual Messengers and
Ministers generally: and, namely, of Blessed Michæl, Blessed
Gabriel, Blessed Raphæl, and Blessed Uriel; and also especially,
of all those, which do appertain unto the Heptarchical Mystery,
theurgically, (as yet) and very briefly unto me declared: under
the method of Seven Mighty Kings, and their Seven Faithful and
Princely Ministers, with their subjects and servants, to them belonging. And in this Thy great Mercy and Grace, on me bestowed, and to me confirmed, (O Almighty God,) Thou shalt,
(to the great comfort of Thy faithful servants,) approve, to Thy
very enemies, and mine, the truth and certainty of Thy manifold, most merciful promises, heretofore, made unto me: And
that Thou art the True and Almighty God, Creator of Heaven
and Earth, (upon whom I do call and in whom I put all my
trust,) and Thy Ministers, to be the true, and faithful Angels of
light: which have, hitherto, principally, and according to Thy

Divine providence dealt with us: And, also, I, thy poor and simple servant, shall then, In and By Thee, be better able to serve Thee, according to Thy well pleasing: to Thy Honour and Glory: Yea, even in these most miserable, and lamentable days. Grant, Oh grant, O our Heavenly Father, grant this, (I pray Thee,) for Thy only begotten Son IESUS CHRIST, His sake: Amen, Amen, Amen.

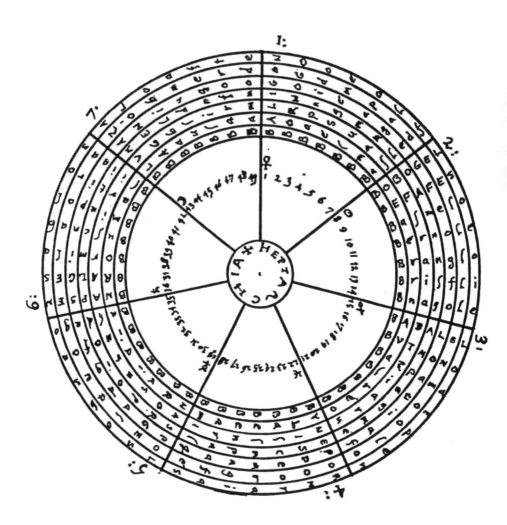

THE TABLE OF THE 49 GOOD ANGELS

# THE DEVOUT AND PIOUS INVITATIONS TO THE GOOD HEPTARCHICAL ANGELS

☙

*§1: The General & Common Exordium & Conclusion Appertaining to the Seven Heptarchical Kings Inviting.*

 PUISSANT AND NOBLE KING, N*., AND BY WHAT Name elssoever thou are called, or mayest truely and duely be called: To Whose peculiar Government, Charge, Disposition, and Kingly Office doth appertain the . . .†

. . . Therefore, In the Name of the King of Kings, the Lord of Hosts, the Almighty GOD, Creator of Heaven and Earth and of all things visible and invisible: O right Noble King, N‡., Come now, and appear, with thy Prince and his ministers and subjects, to my perfect, and sensible eye's judgement: in a goodly and friendly manner, to my comfort and help, for the advancing of the Honour and Glory of our Almighty GOD, by my service: as much as by Thy Wisdom and Power, in thy proper Kingly Office, and Government, I may be helped and enabled unto: Amen. COME, O right Noble King, N‡., I say COME. Amen.

✠Glory be to the Father, to the Sonne, and to the Holy Ghost, as it was in the beginning, is now and ever shall be , world without end, Amen.

\* Insert the name of the King of the day here.
† Insert the office of the King, as given in Chapter Seven.
‡ Insert the name of the King here.
‡ Insert the name of the King.

§2: *The General & Common Exordium & Conclusion appertaining to the Seven Heptarchical Princes Inviting.*

✠O NOBLE PRINCE, N**., AND BY WHAT NAME ELSSOEVER THOU art called, or mayest truely, and duely be called. To whose peculiar Government, Charge, Disposition, Office, and Princely Dignity doth appertain the ... ††

... Therefore, In the Name of Almighty GOD, the King of Kings, And for His Honour, and Glory, to be advanced by my faithful service, I require thee, O Noble Prince, N‡‡., to COME presently, and to show thyself, to my perfect and sensible eye's judgement, with thy Ministers, servants and subjects; to my comfort, and help, in Wisdom, and Power, according to the property of thy noble office: COME, O Noble Prince, N⧎., I say COME, Amen.

✠Our Father who art in heaven, hallowed be Thy Name. Thy kingdom come. Thy will be done on Earth, as it is in Heaven. Give us this day our daily bread. And forgive us our trespasses, as we forgive those who trespass against us. And lead us not into temptation, but deliver us from evil: For Thine is the kingdom, and the power, and the glory, for ever and ever, Amen.

** Insert the name of the Prince here.
†† Insert the office of the Prince as given in Chapter Seven.
‡‡ Insert the name of the Prince here.
⧎ Insert the name of the Prince here.

# SOME RECITAL & CONTESTATION OF THE PECULIAR OFFICES, WORDS, & DEEDS OF THE SEVEN HEPTARCHICAL KINGS & PRINCES

(in their peculiar days to be used).

Ỷ

## SONDAYE
### THE OFFICES OF KING BOBOGEL

\* . . . the distributing, giving, and bestowing of wisdom and science. The teaching of true philosophy, true understanding of all learning, grounded on wisdom, with the excellencies in Nature. And of many other great mysteries, marvelously available and necessary to the advancing of the glory of our God and Creator. And who said to me in respect of these mysteries attaining: "Dee, Dee, Dee, at length but not too late". . .

### THE OFFICES OF PRINCE BORNOGO

. . . the altering of the corruption of Nature in perfection; the knowledge of metals; and generally the princely ministering to the right noble and mighty King Bobogel in his government and distributing, giving, and bestowing of Wisdom, Science, and True Philosophy, and true understanding of all learning, grounded upon wisdom; and of other very many his peculiar royal properties. And who said unto me: *What thou desirest in me shall be fulfilled...*

## MONDAYE
### THE OFFICES OF KING CARMARA

. . .who, in this Heptarchical Doctrine, at Blessed Uriel, his hand, didst receive the golden rod of government and measuring, and the chair of dignity and doctrine, And didst appear first to us, adorned with a triple diadem, in a long purple robe. Who saidst

---

\*I have used the elipsis ( . . . . ) to indicate the beginning and end to the passage. The passages are inserted into the general exordiums given in Chapter Six.

to me͵ at Mortlake͵: *I minister the strength of God unto thee.*
Likewise who saidest: *these mysteries hath God, lastly , and of his
great mercies, granted unto thee.* Thou shalt be glutted, yea filled, yea
thou shalt swell and be puffed up, with perfect knowledge of God's
mysteries in his mercies.* And who saidst: *This Art is to be the further
understanding of all sciences that are past, present, and yet to come.*
And immediately thou didst say unto me: *Kings there are in Nature, with Nature, and above Nature. Thou art dignified.* And who
saidst, concerning the use of the tables: *This is but the first step.
Neither shalt thou practice them in vain.* And, saidst thou generally
of God's mercies and graces on me decreed and bestowed:—
*Whatsoever thou shalt speak, do, or work shall be profitable and ac-
ceptable and in the end shall be good.* . .

### THE OFFICES OF PRINCE HAGONEL

. . . To whose commandment the Sons of Light and their Sons
are subject and are thy servants. To whose power the operation
of the earth is subject. Who are the first of the twelve and whose
seal is called 'Barces'. At whose commandment are the Kings,
Noblemen, and Princes of Nature, who are Primus and Quartus
Hagonel. Who by the seven of the seven (which are the sons
of Æternity) dost work marvels amongst the people of the earth.
And who hast said unto me that I also, by the same, thy servants
should work marvels. Oh Noble Hagonel, who art minister to
the triple crowned King CARMARA, and, notwithstanding art Prince
of these 42 Angels, whose names and characters are here presented.

### THE OFFICES OF KING BLUMAZA§

### THE OFFICES OF PRINCE BRALGES

. . . who saidst the creatures living in thy dominion are͵ subject to thine own power. Whose subject are invisible and which
(to my Seer) appeared like little smokes, without any form, and

§ A blank space is given in the manuscript apparently for some future
insertion. Evidently BLUMAZA and BRALGES are alternate Entities for Monday.

whose seal of government is:

Who saidst: *Behold, I am come. I will teach the names without numbers, the creatures subject unto me shall be known unto you. . .*

## TUESDAYE

### THE OFFICES OF KING BABALEL

. . . who art King in waters, mighty and wonderful in waters; whose power is in the bowels of the waters; whose royal person with the noble Prince Befafes and his 42 ministers, the triple-crowned King CARMARA hath me use to the glory, praise, and honour of him which created you all to the laud and praise of his Majesty . . .

### THE OFFICES OF PRINCE BEFAFES

. . . who are Prince of the seas; thy power is upon the waters; thou drowndest Pharoah and hast destroyed the wicked; thy name was known to Moses; thou livedst in Israel; who hast measured the waters; who wast with King Solomon; and also long after that with Scotus* but not known to him by thy true name, for he called thee Mares. And since thou wast with none; except when thou preservest me through the mercy of God from the power of the wicked; and wast with me in extremity. Thou wast with me thoroughly. Who, of the Ægyptians has been called OBELISON, in respect of thy pleasant deliverance. And by that name to be known and of me noted in record to be the noble and courteous OBELISON; whose noble ministers 42 are of very great power, dignity, and authority. As some in the measuring of the motions of the waters and saltiness of the seas; in giving good success in battles; reducing ships and all manner of vessels that float upon the seas. To some, all the fishes and monsters of the seas, yea, all that live therein are well known; and, generally, are the distributors of God's judgements upon the

* Possibly Duns Scotus, the scholastic philosopher.

waters that cover the earth. Others do beautify Nature in her composition. The rest are distributors and deliverers of treasures and unknown substances of the seas. Thou, Oh noble Prince BEFAFES, hadst me use the name of God . . .

## WEDDENSDAYE
### THE OFFICES OF KING BNASPOL

. . . to whom the earth with her bowels and secrets whatsoever are delivered and hast said to me heretofore what thou art, there I may know. Thou art great, but (as thou truly didst confess) He in whom thou art, is greater than thou. . .

### THE OFFICES OF PRINCE BLISDON

. . . unto whom the keys of the mysteries of the earth are delivered. Whose 42 ministers are Angels that govern under thee. All which thy mighty King BNASPOL bade me use and affirmed that they are and shall be at my commandment . . .

## THURSDAYE
### THE OFFICES OF KING BYNEPOR

. . . upon the distribution of participation of whose exalted most especial and glorified power resteth only and dependeth, the general state of condition of all things. Whose sanctification , glory, and renown, although it had beginning, yet can it not either have ending. He that measureth said and thou wast the End of his workmanship. Thou art like him and of him; yet not as partaking or adherent, but distinct in one degree. When he came thou was magnified by his coming; and are sanctified, world without end.

*The highest life,*
*The best life,*
*The least life is measured in your hands.*

Notwithstanding, thou are not of thyself; neither is thy power thine own. Magnified be His Name. Thou art in all; and all hast some being by thee; yet thy power is nothing in respect of His power which hath sent thee. Thou beginnest new worlds, new people, new kings, and new knowledge of a new government; and hast said to me: *thou shalt work marvelously, marvelously by my workmanship in the Highest* . . .

### THE OFFICES OF PRINCE BUTMONO

. . . who are life and breath in living creatures. All things live by thee, the image of One excepted. All the kinds of beasts of the earth dost thou endue with life. Thy seal is their glory. Of God, thou are sanctified; and thou rejoyceth the living, the end and beginning of all beasts thou knowest; and by sufferance, thou disposest them. . . .

## FRYDAYE

### THE OFFICES OF KING BALIGON

. . . who canst distribute and bestow at pleasure all and whatsoever can be wrought in ærial actions; who hast the government of thyself perfect as a mystery known unto thyself. Who didst advertise me of this stone and holy receptical; both needful to be had; and also didst direct me to the taking of it; being presently and in a few minutes of time brought to my sight (from the secret of the depths, where it was hid, in the uttermost part of the Roman possession); which stone, thou warnest me that no mortal hand but mine own should touch and saidst unto me: *Thou shalt prevail with it, with Kings, and with all the creatures of the world, whose beauty in virtue shall be more worth than the kingdoms of the earth.* For the which purposes here rehearsed and other; partly now to be exercised and enjoyed; and partly hereafter more abundantly (as the Lord God of Hosts shall dispose); and also because thou thyself art governor of the 42 , thy mighty, faithful and obedient ministers† . . .

#### THE OFFICES OF PRINCE BAGENOL§

### SATERDAYE

#### THE OFFICES OF KING BNAPSEN

. . . who saidst unto me that by thee I shall cast out the power of all wicked spirits; and that by thee I shall or may know the doings and practices of evil men; and more than may be spoken or uttered to man . . .

#### THE OFFICES OF PRINCE BRORGES

. . . who, being the Prince, chief minister and governor under the right puissant King BNAPSEN didst (to my Seer) appear in a most terrible manner, with fiery flaming streams and saidst: *I am the Gate of Death. And through the Glory of God I smite the houses of the impious* . . .

† Dee gives two rather lengthy notes, one in English, the other in Latin. The English note merely repeats instruction as to the mounting of the stone on the Sigil of Æmeth, and states, once more, that 'wherein thou shalt at all times behold (privately to thyself) the state of God's people through the whole earth.'

The Latin note translates as follows:—See also the sayings of Ephodius where, concerning Adamanta, in which diverse signs are given for responding to God. See Epiphanius concerning precious stones and their meaning. See his writings concerning the Unim and Thummim. See the book received at Trebonæ. It is written in the books of Epiphanius that the vision that appeared to Moses on the mountain, the laws that were given were expressed in sapphires.

§ None are given.

# BOOK THREE

# THE FORTY-EIGHT ANGELIC KEYS

*Received at Diverse Times from April 13th to July 13th*
*At Cracow, Poland*
*out of the pure mercy of our God to whom alone*
*we offer all praise, honour, and glory, Amen.*

### THE FIRST KEY

| | | | |
|---|---|---|---|
| 1.1 | OL | *Ol* | I |
| 1.2 | SONF | *sonf* | raygne |
| 1.3 | VORSG | *vorsg,* | over you |
| 1.4 | GOHO | *gohó* | sayeth |
| 1.5 | IAD | *Iad* | the God |
| 1.6 | BALT | *balt* | of Justice |
| 1.7 | LANSH | *lansh* | in powre exalted |
| 1.8 | CALZ | *calz* | above the firmaments |
| 1.9 | VONPHO | *vonpho,* | of wrath: |
| 1.10 | SOBRA | *sobra* | in Whose |
| 1.11 | ZOL | *z-ol* | hands |
| 1.12 | ROR | *ror* | the Sonne |
| 1.13 | I | *i* | is |
| 1.14 | TA | *ta* | as |
| 1.15 | NAZPSAD | *nazpsad* | a sword, |
| 1.16 | OD | | and* |
| 1.17 | GRAA | *Graa* | the Moon |
| 1.18 | TA | *ta* | as |
| 1.19 | MALPRG | *Malprg* | a through-thrusting fire |
| 1.20 | DS | *ds* | which |
| 1.21 | HOLQ | *hol-q* | measureth |

* 1.16: OD for 'and' missing in Sloane MS. 3191.

E

| 1.22 QAA | Qa-a | your garments |
| 1.23 NOTHOA | nothóa | in the mydst |
| 1.24 ZIMZ | zimz | of my vestures, |
| 1.25 OD | Od | and |
| 1.26 COMMAH | commah | trussed you together |
| 1.27 TA | ta | as |
| 1.28 NOBLOH | nobloh | the palms |
| 1.29 ZIEN | zien: | of my hands: |
| 1.30 SOBA | Soba | Whose |
| 1.31 THIL | thil | seats |
| 1.32 GNONP | gnonp | I garnished |
| 1.33 PRGE | prge | with the fire |
| 1.34 ALDI | aldi | of gathering |
| 1.35 DS | Ds | and* |
| 1.36 URBS | urbs | beautified |
| 1.37 OBOLEH | óbóleh | your garments† |
| 1.38 GRSAM | grsam: | with admiration, |
| 1.39 CASARM | Casarm | to whom |
| 1.40 OHORELA | ohoréla | I made a law |
| 1.41 CABA | cabá | to govern |
| 1.42 PIR | pir | the holy ones, |
| 1.43 DS | Ds | and |
| 1.44 ZONRENSG | zonrensg | delivered you |
| 1.45 CAB | cab | a rod |
| 1.46 ERM | erm | with‡ |
| 1.47 IADNAH | Jadnah: | the ark of knowledge. |
| 1.48 PILAH | Pilah | Moreover |
| 1.49 FARZM | farzm | you lifted up your voyces |
| 1.50 OD | | and |
| 1.51 ZNRZA | znrza | sware |
| 1.52 ADNA | adna | obedience⁑ |

 * 1.35 & 1.43: Either Enochian should be OD or English should be 'which'
 † The circumflex in Dee's Enochian is actually a brevis in Sl. MS. 3191 and should be pronounced as a short vowel.
 ‡ 1.46: This is the only time in the keys that ERM is glossed as 'with'; this is a probable copying error. ERM is perhaps 'with the ark', with IADNAH as 'knowlegde'; see 30.180: IADNAMAD for 'undefiled knowledge'.
 ⁑ 1.52 to 1.59: Lacuna in Sl. MS. 3191; Dee's English entered as marginalia. The root column gives a probable reconstruction of the Enochian text.

| | | |
|---|---|---|
| 1.53 OD | | and |
| 1.54 GONO | *gono* | faith |
| 1.55 IADPIL | *Iädpil* | to him |
| 1.56 DS | *Ds* | that |
| 1.57 HOM | *hom* | liveth |
| 1.58 OD | | and |
| 1.59 TOH | *tóh* | triumpheth, |
| 1.60 SOBA | *Soba* | whose |
| 1.61 IAOD | | beginning |
| 1.62 IPAM | *Ipam* | is not |
| 1.63 OD | | nor |
| 1.64 UL | *Lu* | ende* |
| 1.65 IPAMIS | *Ipâmis* | can not be, |
| 1.66 DS | *Ds* | which |
| 1.67 LOHOLO | *lóhôlo* | shyneth |
| 1.68 VEP | *vep* | as a flame |
| 1.69 ZOMD | *zomd* | in the myddst |
| 1.70 POAMAL | *Poamal* | of your pallace |
| 1.71 OD | *od* | and |
| 1.72 SONF | *bogpa* | rayngneth |
| 1.73 AAI | *aäl* | amongst you |
| 1.74 TA | *ta* | as |
| 1.75 PIAP | *piap* | the ballance |
| 1.76 BALTOH | *piamos* | of righteousnes, |
| 1.77 OD | *od* | and |
| 1.78 VAOAN | *vaoan* | truth: |
| 1.79 ZACAR | *ZACARe* | Move |
| 1.80 CA | *c-a* | therfore, |
| 1.81 OD | *od* | and |
| 1.82 ZAMRAN | *ZAMRAN* | shew yourselves: |
| 1.83 ODO | *odo* | open |
| 1.84 CICLE | *cicle* | the Mysteries |
| 1.85 QAA | *Qaa* | of your Creation: |

* 1.64: Dee made a copying error here. Royal Appendix clearly shows UL rather than LU. This is a curious error, because the 'L' prefix in Enochian means 'first', more or less an opposite to the 'end' that is intended. (See 5.46: ULS for 'end'.)

EE

| 1.86 | ZORGE | *zorge,* | Be friendly unto me: |
| 1.87 | LAP | *lap* | for |
| 1.88 | ZIRDO | *zirdo* | I am* |
| 1.89 | NOCO | *noco* | the servant |
| 1.90 | MAD | *MAD* | of the same your God: |
| 1.91 | HOATH | *Hoath* | the true Worshipper |
| 1.92 | IAIDA | *Jaida.* | of the Highest. |

### THE SECOND KEY

☿

| 2.1 | ADGT | *Adgt* | Can |
| 2.2 | UPAAH | *v-pa-âh* | the wings |
| 2.3 | ZONG | *zongom* | of the windes† |
| 2.4 | OM | | |
| 2.5 | FAAIP | *ſa-á-ip* | understand |
| 2.6 | SALD | *sald* | your voyces of wonder |
| 2.7 | VIV | *vi-iv* | O you the second‡ |
| 2.8 | L | *L* | of the first, |
| 2.9 | SOBAM | *sobam* | Whome |
| 2.10 | IALPRG | *Iál-prg* | the burning flames |
| 2.11 | IZAZAZ | *I-zâ-zaz* | have framed |
| 2.12 | PIADPH | *pi-ádph* | within the depths of my Jaws, |
| 2.13 | CASARMA | *Cas-arma* | whome |
| 2.14 | ABRAMG | *abramg* | I have prepared |
| 2.15 | TA | *ta* | as |
| 2.16 | TALHO | *talho* | Cupps |
| 2.17 | PARACLEDA | *paráclêda* | for a wedding |
| 2.18 | Q | *Q-ta* | or |
| 2.19 | TA | | as |
| 2.20 | LORSLQ | *lors-l-q* | the flowres |

    * 1.88: Possible copying error. ZIR appears as 'I am' in 2.53, 3.4 & 4.46, while ZIRDO appears as 'I am' only in this passage in Royal Appendix. If so the ZIRDO error was repeated in most of the later calls. Note that DONOCO would be linguistically similar to CNOQUO in 21.35, 17.34, & 18.38. The correct passage may be ZIR DONOCO or ZIR CNOQUO rather than ZIRDO NOCO.

    † 2.3 to 2.6: A little confusion here in Dee's matching. OM should be 'understand' (see 7.53, 10.54, 16.19, & 30.113). Thus ZONG is 'of the winds', FAAIP is 'your voices', and SALD is 'of wonder'.

    ‡ 2.7: Is Dee's double 'i' in VI-IV an error or a variation? See 4.13, 5.33, 6.34, & 16.2 for VIV as 'second'.

| | | | |
|---|---|---|---|
| 2.21 | TURBS | *turbs* | in their beawty |
| 2.22 | OOGE | *ōoge* | for the Chamber |
| 2.23 | BALTOH | *Baltoh* | of righteousnes |
| 2.24 | GIUI | *Giui* | Stronger |
| 2.25 | CHIS | *chis* | are |
| 2.26 | LUSD | *Lusd* | your fete |
| 2.27 | ORRI | *orri* | then the barren stone: |
| 2.28 | OD | *Od* | And |
| 2.29 | MICALP | *micalp* | myghtier |
| 2.30 | CHIS | *chís* | are |
| 2.31 | BIA | *bia* | your voices |
| 2.32 | OZONGON | *ózŏngon* | then the manifold windes. |
| 2.33 | LAP | *Lap* | For |
| 2.34 | NOAN | *noán* | you are become |
| 2.35 | TROF | *trof* | a buylding |
| 2.36 | CORS | *cors* | such |
| 2.37 | TA | *ta* | as |
| 2.38 | GE | *ge,* | is not |
| 2.39 | OQ | *o-q* | but |
| 2.40 | MANIN | *manin* | in the mynde |
| 2.41 | IAIDON | *Ja-i-don:* | of the all powerfull. |
| 2.42 | TORZU | *Torzu* | Arrise |
| 2.43 | GOHEL | *góhel* | sayeth the First |
| 2.44 | ZACAR | *ZACAR* | Move |
| 2.45 | CA | *ca* | therefore |
| 2.46 | CNOQOD | *c-nó-qod,* | unto his Servants: |
| 2.47 | ZAMRAN | *ZAMRAN* | Shew yourselves |
| 2.48 | MICALZO | *micalzo* | in powre: |
| 2.49 | OD | *od* | And |
| 2.50 | OZAZM | *ozazm* | make me |
| 2.51 | VRELP | *vrelp* | a strong Seething:‡ |
| 2.52 | LAP | *Lap* | for |
| 2.53 | ZIR | *zir* | I am |
| 2.54 | IOIAD | *Ioiad.* | of him that liveth forever. |

‡ 2.51: The English 'Seething' is often modernized into 'Seer' or 'Seer of Things'. More likely 'Seething' is a gerund of 'to seeth'; See the Oxford English Dictionary entry on 'Seething'.

## THE THIRD KEY

♑

| | | | |
|---|---|---|---|
| 3.1 | MICMA | *Micma* | Behold |
| 3.2 | GOHO | *gohó* | sayeth |
| 3.3 | IAD | *Piad* | your God, |
| 3.4 | ZIR | *zir* | I am |
| 3.5 | COMSELH | *cómselh* | a Circle |
| 3.6 | AZIEN | *azien* | on Whose hands |
| 3.7 | BIAB | *biab* | stand |
| 3.8 | OS | *Os* | 12 |
| 3.9 | LONDOH | *Lón-doh* | Kingdoms. |
| 3.10 | NORZ | *Norz* | Six |
| 3.11 | CHIS | *chis* | are |
| 3.12 | OTHIL | *óthil* | the seats |
| 3.13 | GIGIPAH | *Gigípah* | of living breath, |
| 3.14 | UNDL | *und-l* | the rest |
| 3.15 | CHIS | *chis* | are |
| 3.16 | TA | *tá* | as |
| 3.17 | PUIM | *pû-im* | sharp sickles: |
| 3.18 | Q | *Q* | or |
| 3.19 | MOSPLEH | *mos-pleh* | the horns |
| 3.20 | TELOCH | *teloch* | of death |
| 3.21 | QUIIN | *Qui-i-n* | wherein |
| 3.22 | TOLTORG | *toltorg* | the Creatures of the earth |
| 3.23 | CHIS | *chis* | are, |
| 3.24 | ICHISGE | *i-chis-ge* | to are not*, |
| 3.25 | M | *m* | Except |
| 3.26 | OZIEN | *ozíen* | myne own hand, |
| 3.27 | DS | *dst* | which§ |
| 3.28 | BRGDA | *brgda* | slepe |
| 3.29 | OD | *od* | and |
| 3.30 | TORZUL | *torzul* | shall ryse. |
| 3.31 | ILI | *í-lí* | In the first |

* 3.24: The English is a bit confsed here. ICHISGE probably means-
'I am not'.

§ 3.27: 'T' in '*dst*' probably accidental, although '*dst*' as 'which' appears
at 4.28. Ds is glossed as 'which' everywhere else.

| 3.32 | EOL | *E-ól* | I made you |
|------|-----|--------|------------|
| 3.33 | BALZARG | *balzarg* | stuards |
| 3.34 | OD | *od* | and |
| 3.35 | AALA | *áâla* | placed you |
| 3.36 | THILN | *Thiln* | in seats |
| 3.37 | OS | *os* | 12 |
| 3.38 | NETAAB | *ne-tâ-ab,* | of government, |
| 3.39 | DLUGA | *dluga* | giving |
| 3.40 | VOMZARG | *vomsarg* | unto every one of you |
| 3.41 | LONSA | *Lonsa* | powre |
| 3.42 | CAPIMALI | *Cap-mi-áli* | successively* |
| 3.43 | VORS | *vors* | over |
| 3.44 | CLA | *cla* | 456, |
| 3.45 | HOMIL | *homil* | the true ages |
| 3.46 | COCASB | *cocasb* | of tyme, |
| 3.47 | FAFEN | *fafen* | to the intent that, |
| 3.48 | IZIZOP | *izízop* | from your highest vessells |
| 3.49 | OD | *od* | and |
| 3.50 | MIINOAG | *miinôag* | the Corners |
| 3.51 | DE | *de* | of |
| 3.52 | GNETAAB | *gne-tâab* | your governments, |
| 3.53 | VAUN | *vaun* | you might work |
| 3.54 | NANÆEL | *na-ná-ê-el* | my powre: |
| 3.55 | PANPIR | *panpir* | powring downe |
| 3.56 | MALPIRGI | *Malpirgi* | the fires of life and encrease, |
| 3.57 | PILD | *caósg* | continually |
| 3.58 | CAOSG | *Pild* | on the earth |
| 3.59 | NOAN | *noan* | Thus you are become |
| 3.60 | UNALAH | *vnalah* | the skirts |
| 3.61 | BALT | *balt* | of Justice |
| 3.62 | OD | *od* | and |
| 3.63 | VOOAN | *vooán* | Truth. |
| 3.64 | DOOIAP | *do-ó-î-ap* | In the name |
| 3.65 | MAD | *MAD* | of the same. your God |
| 3.66 | GOHOLOR | *Gohólor* | Lift up, |

* 3.42; CAPIMALI rather than CAPMIALI; see 30.122. Also see 4.30 for root CAPIM-.

| 3.67 | GOHUS | gohús | I say, |
| 3.68 | AMIRAN | amiran | yourselves. |
| 3.69 | MICMA | Mícma, | Behold |
| 3.70 | IEHUSOZ | Iehúsoz | his mercies |
| 3.71 | CACACOM | ca-cá-com | florish |
| 3.72 | OD | od | and |
| 3.73 | DOOAIN | do-o-â-in | Name |
| 3.74 | NOAR | noar | is become |
| 3.75 | MICAOLZ | mi-cá-olz | mighty |
| 3.76 | AAIOM | a-aí-om | amongst us |
| 3.77 | CASARMG | Casármg | In whom |
| 3.78 | GOHIA | gohia | we say |
| 3.79 | ZACAR | ZACAR | Move*, |
| 3.80 | UNIGLAG | vníglag | Descend |
| 3.81 | OD | od | and |
| 3.82 | IMUAMAR | Im-uâ-mar | apply yourselves unto us |
| 3.83 | PUGO | pugo | as unto |
| 3.84 | PLAPLI | plapli | partakers |
| 3.85 | ANANÆL | anánæl | of the secret wisdom |
| 3.86 | QAAN | Qáan. | of your Creation. |

### THE FOURTH KEY

☿

| 4.1 | OTHIL | Othíl | I have set |
| 4.2 | LASDI | lasdi | my fete |
| 4.3 | BABAGE | babâge | in the Sowth |
| 4.4 | OD | od | and |
| 4.5 | DORPHA | dorpha | have loked abowt me |
| 4.6 | GOHOL | Gohól | sayng, |
| 4.7 | GCHISGE | G-chisge | are not |
| 4.8 | AVAVAGO | avávâgo | the Thunders of encrease |
| 4.9 | CORMP | Cormp | numbred |
| 4.10 | PD | pd | 33, |
| 4.11 | DS | dsonf | which |
| 4.12 | SONF | | rayne |
| 4.13 | VIV | viv-di-v | in the second |
| 4.14 | DIU | | Angle, |

* 3.79: Alternate pronunciation given as zod-a-car.

| 4.15 | CASARMI | Casármi | under whom |
| 4.16 | OALI | Oali | I have placed |
| 4.17 | MAPM | Mapm | 9639 |
| 4.18 | SOBAM | Sobam | Whome |
| 4.19 | AG | ag | None |
| 4.20 | CORMPO | cormpó | hath yet numbred, |
| 4.21 | CRIP | c-rp-l | but* |
| 4.22 | L | | one, |
| 4.23 | CASARMG | Casarmg | in whome |
| 4.24 | CROODZI | croódzi | the second beginning of things |
| 4.25 | CHIS | chis | are |
| 4.26 | OD | od | and |
| 4.27 | UGEG | vgeg | wax strong |
| 4.28 | DS | dst | which |
| 4.29 | T | | allso |
| 4.30 | CAPIMAI I | capimáli | successively |
| 4.31 | CHIS | chis | are |
| 4.32 | CAPIMAON | Capimaon | the number of time: |
| 4.33 | OD | od | and |
| 4.34 | LONSHIN | lonshin | their powres |
| 4.35 | CHIS | chis | are |
| 4.36 | TA | ta | as |
| 4.37 | LO | Lo | the first |
| 4.38 | CLA | Cla | 456: |
| 4.39 | TORZU | Torgú | Arrise, |
| 4.40 | NOR | Nor | you sonns |
| 4.41 | QUASAHI | quasáhi | of pleasure, |
| 4.42 | OD | od | and |
| 4.43 | F | F | viset |
| 4.44 | CAOSGA | caósga | the earth: |
| 4.45 | BAGLE | Bagle | for |
| 4.46 | ZIR | Zirendiad | I am† |
| 4.47 | ENAY | | the Lord |
| 4.48 | IAD | | your God, |

* 4.21: CRIP for 'but'; see 10.84.
† 4.46 to 4.48: Zirenaiad may be a contraction: ZIR-ENAY-IAD or 'I am' -'Lord'-'God'.

| 4.49 | DS | Dsi | which |
|---|---|---|---|
| 4.50 | I | | is, |
| 4.51 | OD | od | and |
| 4.52 | APILA | Apíla | liveth. |
| 4.53 | DOOAIP | Do-ó-â-io | In the name |
| 4.54 | QAAL | Q-á-al | of the Creator |
| 4.55 | ZACAR | ZACAR | Move, |
| 4.56 | OD | od | and |
| 4.57 | ZAMRAN | ZAMRAN | shew yourselves |
| 4.58 | OBELISONG | Obelisong | as pleasant deliverers |
| 4.59 | RESTEL | rest-el | That you may praise him |
| 4.60 | AAI | aaf | amongst* |
| 4.61 | NOR | Nor-mô-lap | the sonnes† |
| 4.62 | MOLAP | | of men. |

### THE FIFTH KEY

☿

| 5.1 | SAPAH | Sapáh | The mighty sounds |
|---|---|---|---|
| 5.2 | ZIMII | zímii | have entered‡ |
| 5.3 | D | du-i-v | into the third |
| 5.4 | DIV | | angle, |
| 5.5 | OD | od | and |
| 5.6 | NOAS | noas | are become |
| 5.7 | TA | ta | as |
| 5.8 | QANIS | qa-a-nis | olives |
| 5.9 | ADROCH | adroch | in the olive mount |
| 5.10 | DORPHAL | dorphal | looking with gladnes |
| 5.11 | CAOSG | ca-ósg | upon the earth |
| 5.12 | OD | od | and |
| 5.13 | FAONTS | faonts | dwelling |
| 5.14 | PERIPSOL | péripsol | in the brightnes of the heavens |
| 5.15 | TA | tablior | as |
| 5.16 | BLIOR | | continuall comfortors, |
| 5.17 | CASARM | Casarm | unto whom |
| 5.18 | AMIPZI | amipzi | I fastened |

* 4.60: Copying error by Dee. AA for 'amongst'; see 1.73; 7.52, 7.6 &c.
† 4.61 to 4.62: MOLAP for 'of men', because NOR is 'sons'; see 4.40.
‡ 5.2 to 5.3: D for third; see 6.36, 7.33, 17.2. DIV for 'angle'; see 4.14, 6.3

| 5.19 | NAZ | *nazarth* | pillers§ |
| 5.20 | ARTH | | of gladnes |
| 5.21 | AF | *af* | 19 |
| 5.22 | OD | *od* | and |
| 5.23 | DLUGAR | *dlugar* | gave them |
| 5.24 | ZIZOP | *zizop* | vessels |
| 5.25 | ZLIDA | *z-lida* | to water |
| 5.26 | CAOSGI | *caósgi* | the earth |
| 5.27 | TOLTORGI | *toltórgi* | with her creatures, |
| 5.28 | OD | *od* | and |
| 5.29 | ZCHIS | *z-chis* | they are |
| 5.30 | ESIASCH | *esíasch* | the brothers |
| 5.31 | L | *L* | of the first |
| 5.32 | OD | *taviu* | and* |
| 5.33 | VIV | | second |
| 5.34 | OD | *od* | and |
| 5.35 | IAOD | *iáod* | the beginning |
| 5.36 | THILD | *thild* | of their own seats |
| 5.37 | DS | *ds* | which |
| 5.38 | PERAL | | are garnished† |
| 5.39 | HUBAR | *hubar* | with continually burning lamps |
| 5.40 | PEOAL | *Peóal* | 69636 |
| 5.41 | SOBA | *soba* | whose |
| 5.42 | CORMFA | *cormfa* | numbers |
| 5.43 | CHIS | *chis* | are |
| 5.44 | TA | *ta* | as |
| 5.45 | LA | *la* | the first |
| 5.46 | ULS | *vls* | the endes |
| 5.47 | OD | *od* | and |
| 5.48 | QCOCASB | *Q-có-casb* | the contents of tyme. |
| 5.49 | CA | *Ca* | Therefore |
| 5.50 | NIIS | *niis* | Come you |
| 5.51 | OD | *od* | and |

§ 5.19: NAZ as 'pillars'; see 8.7 NAZ- root for 'pillars'.

* 5.32: OD for 'and'; *ta* probably a copying error.

† 5.38 to 5.39: Lacuna in Sl. MS. 3191. Dee wrote the English as marginalia. See Royal Appendix (or *True Relation*) on July 5, 1584, the spirit Nalvage instructs that the word PERAL be added. Dee evidently neglected to do so when compiling Sl. MS. 3191.

| 5.52 | DARBS | *Darbs* | obey |
| 5.53 | QAAS | *Q-á-as* | your creation, |
| 5.54 | F | *Feth-ar-zi* | viset us* |
| 5.55 | ETHARZI | | in peace |
| 5.56 | OD | *od* | and |
| 5.57 | BLIOR | *blióra* | comfort |
| 5.58 | IAIAL | *ia-ial* | Conclude us |
| 5.59 | EDNAS | *ed-nas* | as receivers |
| 5.60 | CICLES | *cicles* | of your mysteries: |
| 5.61 | BAGLE | *Bágle* | for why? |
| 5.62 | IAD | *Geiad* | Our Lord and Mr. |
| 5.63 | I | *i-L* | is |
| 5.64 | L | | all one. |

## THE SIXTH KEY

♉

| 6.1 | GAH | *Gah* | The spirits |
| 6.2 | S | *s* | of ye 4th |
| 6.3 | DIU | *díu* | Angle |
| 6.4 | CHIS | *chis* | are |
| 6.5 | EM | *em* | Nine, |
| 6.6 | MICAOLZ | *micálzo* | Mighty‡ |
| 6.7 | PILZIN | *pilzin* | in the firmaments of waters, |
| 6.8 | SOBAM | *sobam* | Whome |
| 6.9 | EL | *El* | the first |
| 6.10 | HARG | *harg* | hath planted |
| 6.11 | MIR | *mir* | a torment |
| 6.12 | BABALON | *babálon* | to the wicked |
| 6.13 | OD | *od* | and |
| 6.14 | OBLOC | *obloc* | a garland |
| 6.15 | SAMVELG | *samvelg* | to the righteous |
| 6.16 | DLUGAR | *dlugar* | giving unto them |
| 6.17 | MALPRG | *marprg* | fyrie darts |
| 6.18 | AR | *arcaósgi* | to vanne |
| 6.19 | CAOSGI | | the earth |
| 6.20 | OD | *od* | and |

* 5.54: F for 'visit'; see 4.43, 6.25.

‡ 6.6: MICAOLZ for 'mighty'; see 3.74, 18.2, 30.6.

| | | | |
|---|---|---|---|
| 6.21 | ACAM | *Acám* | 7699 |
| 6.22 | CANAL | *canal* | continuall Workmen |
| 6.23 | SOBA | *sobólzar* | whose† |
| 6.24 | ELZAP | | courses |
| 6.25 | F | *f-bliard* | viset |
| 6.26 | BLIARD | | with comfort |
| 6.27 | CAOSG | *caosgi* | the earth |
| 6.28 | OD | *od* | and |
| 6.29 | CHIS | *chis* | are |
| 6.30 | ANETAB | *anétab* | in government |
| 6.31 | OD | *od* | and |
| 6.32 | MAIM | *miam* | contynuance |
| 6.33 | TA | *ta* | as |
| 6.34 | VIV | *viv* | the second |
| 6.35 | OD | *od* | and |
| 6.36 | D | *d* | the third |
| 6.37 | DARSAR | *Darsar* | Wherefore |
| 6.38 | SOLPETH | *sol-peth* | hearken unto |
| 6.39 | BIEN | *bien* | my voyce |
| 6.40 | BRITA | *Brita* | I have talked of you |
| 6.41 | OD | *od* | and |
| 6.42 | ZACAM | *zácam* | I move you |
| 6.43 | GMICALZO | *g-micálzo* | in power and presence, |
| 6.44 | SOBA | *sob-há-ath* | whose |
| 6.45 | HAATH | | works |
| 6.46 | TRIAN | *trían* | shall be |
| 6.47 | LUIAHE | *Lu-iá-he* | a song of honor |
| 6.48 | OD | *odecrin* | and |
| 6.49 | ECRIN | | the praise |
| 6.50 | MAD | *MAD* | of your God |
| 6.51 | QAAON | *Q-a-a-on* | in your Creation. |

### THE SEVENTH KEY

☿

| | | | |
|---|---|---|---|
| 7.1 | RAAS | *Raas* | The East |
| 7.2 | I | *isâlman* | is |

† 6.23 to 6.24: SOBA for 'whose'; see 1.30, 1.60, 5.41, 7.27, &c. ELZAP for 'courses'; see 30.62.

| 7.3 | SALMAN | | a howse |
|------|--------|--------|---------|
| 7.4 | PARADIZ | *paradiz* | of virgins§ |
| 7.5 | ŒCRIMI | *oécrîmi* | singing praises |
| 7.6 | AAI | *aao* | amongst* |
| 7.7 | IALPIRGAH | *ial-pîrgah* | the flames of the first glory,† |
| 7.8 | QUIIN | *qui-in* | wherein |
| 7.9 | ENAY | *enay* | the Lord |
| 7.10 | BUTMON | *butmon* | hath opened his mouth |
| 7.11 | OD | *od* | and |
| 7.12 | INOAS | *inóas* | they are become |
| 7.13 | NI | *ni* | 28 |
| 7.14 | PARADIAL | *paradíal* | Living dwellings |
| 7.15 | CASARMG | *casarmg* | in whom |
| 7.16 | UGEAR | *vgéar* | the strength of men |
| 7.17 | CHIRLAN | *chirlan* | rejoyceth |
| 7.18 | OD | *od* | and |
| 7.19 | ZONAC | *zonac* | they are apparcled |
| 7.20 | LUCIFTIAN | *Luciftian* | with ornaments of brightnes |
| 7.21 | CORS | *cors* | such |
| 7.22 | TA | *ta* | as |
| 7.23 | VAUL | *vaul* | work |
| 7.24 | ZIRN | *zirn* | wonders |
| 7.25 | TOL | *tol-hâ-mi* | on all |
| 7.26 | HAMI | | creatures |
| 7.27 | SOBA | *soba* | Whose |
| 7.28 | LONDOH | *londóh* | Kingdoms |
| 7.29 | OD | *od* | and |
| 7.30 | MIAM | *miam* | continuance |
| 7.31 | CHIS | *chis* | are |
| 7.32 | TA | *tad* | as |
| 7.33 | D | | the third |
| 7.34 | OD | *o* | and |
| 7.35 | ES | *dés* | fourth |
| 7.36 | UMADEA | *vmádêa* | strong towres |
| 7.37 | OD | *od* | and |

§ 7.4: Alternate pronunciation *'paradizod'*.
* 7.6: An for 'amongst'; see 1.73, 7.52, 12.22, 13.25, &c.
† 7.7: Contraction of IALPRG–GAH or 'burning flame'–'spirit'.

| 7.38 | PIBLIAR | *pibliar* | places of comfort |
|------|---------|-----------|-------------------|
| 7.39 | OTHIL | *Othilrit* | The seats* |
| 7.40 | RIT | | of mercy |
| 7.41 | OD | *od* | and |
| 7.42 | MIAM | *miám* | continuance. |
| 7.43 | CNOQUOL | *Cnoquol* | O you Servants |
| 7.44 | RIT | *Rit* | of Mercy, |
| 7.45 | ZACAR | *ZACAR,* | Move, |
| 7.46 | ZAMRAN | *ZAMRAN* | Appeare, |
| 7.47 | ŒCRIMI | *oëcrimi* | sing praises |
| 7.48 | QAADAH | *q-a-dah* | unto the Creator: |
| 7.49 | OD | *od* | And |
| 7.50 | OMICAOLZ | *omicaolz* | be mighty† |
| 7.51 | AAIOM | *aaiom* | amongst us |
| 7.52 | BAGLE | *Bagle* | For |
| 7.53 | PAPBOR | *papnor* | to this remembrance |
| 7.54 | IDLUGAM | *idlúgam* | is given |
| 7.55 | LONSHI | *lonshi* | powre |
| 7.56 | OD | *od* | and |
| 7.57 | UMPLIF | *vmplif* | our strength |
| 7.58 | UGEG | *vgêgi* | waxeth strong |
| 7.59 | BIGLIAD | *Bigliad* | in our Comforter. |

### THE EIGHTH KEY

ᛯ

| 8.1 | BAZME | *Bazmêlo* | The Midday |
|-----|-------|-----------|------------|
| 8.2 | LO | | the first‡ |
| 8.3 | I | *i* | is |
| 8.4 | TA | *ta* | as |
| 8.5 | PIRIPSON | *pirípson* | the third heaven |
| 8.6 | OLN | *oln* | made |
| 8.7 | NAZ | *nazâvábh* | of Hiacynth Pillers |
| 8.8 | AVABH | | |
| 8.9 | OX | *ox* | 26 |
| 8.10 | CASARMG | *casarmg* | in whome |

* 7.39 to 7.40: OTHIL for 'seats'; see 3.12. RIT for 'Mercy'; see 7.44.
† 7.50: Alternate pronunciation: *Omicaolzod.*
‡ 8.2: Lo as 'first'; see 4.37.

| 8.11 URAN | *Vrán* | the Elders |
| 8.12 CHIS | *chis* | are |
| 8.13 UGEG | *vgeg* | become strong |
| 8.14 DS | *dsa-bramg* | which |
| 8.15 ABRAMG | | I have prepared§ |
| 8.16 BALTOHA | *baltôha* | for my own righteousnes |
| 8.17 GOHO | *gohó* | sayth |
| 8.18 IAD | *i̇-ad* | the Lord |
| 8.19 SOBA | *soba* | whose |
| 8.20 MIAM | *miam* | long contynuance* |
| 8.21 TRIAN | *trian* | shall be |
| 8.22 TA | *ta* | as |
| 8.23 LOLCIS | *lól-cis* | bucklers |
| 8.24 ABAI | *Abaíuônin* | to the stowping |
| 8.25 VOVIN | | Dragons† |
| 8.26 OD | *od* | and |
| 8.27 AZIAGIER | *aziágíer* | like unto the harvest |
| 8.28 RIOR | *rior* | of a wyddow. |
| 8.29 IRGIL | *Irgil* | How many |
| 8.30 CHIS | *chís* | are |
| 8.31 DA | *da* | there |
| 8.32 DS | *ds* | which |
| 8.33 PAAOX | *pá-â-ox* | remayn |
| 8.34 BUSD | *busd* | in the glorie |
| 8.35 CAOSGO | *caósgo* | of the earth |
| 8.36 DS | *ds* | which |
| 8.37 CHIS | *chis* | are |
| 8.38 OD | *odípûran* | and |
| 8.39 IPURAN | | shall not see |
| 8.40 TELOCH | *téloâh* | death‡ |
| 8.41 CACARG | *cacarg* | untyll |

§ 8.15: ABRAMG for 'I have prepared'; see 2.14, 11.33.
* 8.20: MIAM for 'long continuance'; see 6.32, 7.30, 7.42. MIAN as '3663'; see 12.61. Dee's error makes the Enochian gibberish.
† 8.25: VOVIN is the stem for 'dragon'; see 8.46 and note to 30.133. The entire passage is idomatic in Enochian; what is probably meant is 'The Lord will be a shield against threatening dragons [devils]'.
‡ 8.40: TELOCH for 'death'; see 3.20, 11.19 and note on 30.133.

| 8.42 | O | O | this |
|------|---|---|------|
| 8.43 | SALMAN | isâlman | howse |
| 8.44 | LONCHO | loncho | fall |
| 8.45 | OD | od | and |
| 8.46 | VOVINA | Vouína | the Dragon |
| 8.47 | CARBAF | carbaf | synck. |
| 8.48 | NIISO | Niíso | Come away, |
| 8.49 | BAGLE | Bagle | for |
| 8.50 | AVAVAGO | aváuâgo | the Thunders |
| 8.51 | GOHON | gohón | have spoken: |
| 8.52 | NIISO | Niíso | Come away, |
| 8.53 | BAGLE | bagle | for |
| 8.54 | MOMAO | mómâo | the Crownes |
| 8.55 | SIAION | siáion | of the Temple |
| 8.56 | OD | od | and |
| 8.57 | MABZA | mábza | the coat |
| 8.58 | IADOIASMOMAR | | |
| | | Jad-oiás-mômar | |
| | | | of him that is, was, and shall be crowned‡ |
| 8.59 | POILP | poilp | are divided |
| 8.60 | NIIS | Niis | Come |
| 8.61 | ZAMRAN | ZAMARN | Appeare |
| 8.62 | CIAOFI | ciaofi | to the terror |
| 8.63 | CAOSGO | caósgo | of the earth |
| 8.64 | OD | od | and |
| 8.65 | BLIORS | bliors | to our comfort |
| 8.66 | OD | od | and |
| 8.67 | CORSI | corsi | of such |
| 8.68 | TA | ta | as |
| 8.69 | ABRAMIG | a-brâmig | are prepared. |

### THE NINTH KEY

♃

| 9.1 | MICAOLI | Mi-cá-ôli | A mighty |
|-----|---------|-----------|----------|
| 9.2 | BRANSG | bransg | garde |

‡ 8.58: Contraction of IAD-I-AS-MOMAR or 'God'-'is'-'was'-'crowned'. See 8.54 for MOMA- root.

F

| 9.3 | PURGEL | *prgel* | of fire |
| 9.4 | NAPTA | *napta* | with two-edged swords |
| 9.5 | IALPOR | *ialpor* | flaming |
| 9.6 | DS | *ds* | (which |
| 9.7 | BRIN | *brin* | have |
| 9.8 | EFAFAFE | *efáfáfe* | viols§ |
| 9.9 | P | *P* | :8: |
| 9.10 | VONPHO | *vonpho* | of wrath |
| 9.11 | OLANI | *oláni* | for two tymes |
| 9.12 | OD | *od* | and |
| 9.13 | OBZA | *obza* | a half: |
| 9.14 | SOBA | *sobca* | whose* |
| 9.15 | UPAAH | *vpâah* | wings |
| 9.16 | CHIS | *chis* | are |
| 9.17 | TATAN | *tatan* | of wormwood, |
| 9.18 | OD | *od* | and |
| 9.19 | TRANAN | *tranan* | of the marrow |
| 9.20 | BALYE | *balye* | of salt,) |
| 9.21 | ALAR | *alar* | have setled |
| 9.22 | LUSDA | *lusda* | their feete |
| 9.23 | SOBOLN | *sobôln* | in the West, |
| 9.24 | OD | *od* | and |
| 9.25 | CHIS | *chís* | are |
| 9.26 | HOLQ | *hôlq* | measured |
| 9.27 | CNOQUODI | *Cnoquódi* | with their Ministers |
| 9.28 | CIAI | *cial* | 9996. |
| 9.29 | UNAL | *vnál* | These |
| 9.30 | ALDON | *aldon* | gather up |
| 9.31 | MOM | *mom* | the moss |
| 9.32 | CAOSGO | *caósgo* | of the earth |
| 9.33 | TA | *ta* | as |
| 9.34 | LAS | *las* | the rich |
| 9.35 | OLLOR | *óllor* | man |
| 9.36 | GNAY | *gnay* | doth |

§ 9.8: English 'viols' usually modernized as 'vials'; possible alternate would be 'violins'. See Oxford English Dictionary on 'viols'.

* 9.14: SOBA as 'whose'; see 1.30, 1.60, 5.41, 6.23, &c. SOBCA appears twice in total, both times in this key.

| 9.37 | LIMLAL | *limlal* | his threasor: |
| 9.38 | AMMA | *Amma* | Cursed |
| 9.39 | CHIIS | *chiis* | ar they |
| 9.40 | SOBA | *sobca* | whose |
| 9.41 | MADRID | *madrid* | iniquities |
| 9.42 | ZCHIS | *zchis,* | they are§ |
| 9.43 | OOANOAN | *oöánôan* | in their eyes |
| 9.44 | CHIS | *chis* | are |
| 9.45 | AVINY | *auíny* | milstones |
| 9.46 | DRILPI | *drilpi* | greater |
| 9.47 | CAOSGI | *caósgin,* | then the earth |
| 9.48 | OD | *od* | And |
| 9.49 | BUTMONI | *butmôni* | from their mowthes |
| 9.50 | PARM | *parm* | rune |
| 9.51 | ZUMVI | *zumvi* | seas |
| 9.52 | CNILA | *Cníla* | of blud: |
| 9.53 | DAZIZ | *Dazis* | Their heds |
| 9.54 | ETHAMZ | *ethámz* | are covered* |
| 9.55 | ACHILDAO | *a-chíldao* | with diamond: |
| 9.56 | OD | *od* | and |
| 9.57 | MIRC | *mirc* | uppon |
| 9.58 | OZOL | *ózól* | their heds |
| 9.59 | CHIS | *chis* | are |
| 9.60 | PIDIAI | *pidiai* | marble |
| 9.61 | COLLAL | *collal* | sleves. |
| 9.62 | ULCININ | *vlcínin* | Happie is he, |
| 9.63 | ASOBAM | *a-sóbam* | on whome |
| 9.64 | UCIM | *vcim* | they frown not. |
| 9.65 | BAGLE | *Bagle* | For why? |
| 9.66 | IAD | *Iadbáltoh* | The God |
| 9.67 | BALTOH | | of righteousnes,† |
| 9.68 | CHIRLAN | *chirlan* | reioyceth |
| 9.69 | PAR | *par* | in them. |
| 9.70 | NIISO | *Níſso* | Come away |
| 9.71 | OD | *od* | and |

§ 9.42: Alternate pronunciation: *Zodchis.*
* 9.54: Alternate pronunciation: *ethamzod.*
† 9.67: BALTOH for 'righteousness'; see 1.76, 2.23.

Ff

| 9.72 | IP | *ip* | not |
| 9.73 | EFAFAFE | *ofáfâfe* | your Viols |
| 9.74 | BAGLE | *Bagle* | For |
| 9.75 | COCASB | *acócasb* | the tyme |
| 9.76 | I | *icórsca* | is‡ |
| 9.77 | CORS | | such |
| 9.78 | TA | | as |
| 9.79 | UNIG | *vnig* | requireth |
| 9.80 | BLIOR | *blior.* | comfort. |

## THE TENTH KEY

🜃

| 10.1 | CORAXO | *Coráxo* | The Thunders of Judgement and Wrath |
| 10.2 | CHIS | *chis* | are |
| 10.3 | CORMP | *cormp* | numbred |
| 10.4 | OD | *od* | and |
| 10.5 | BLANS | *blans* | are haborowed |
| 10.6 | LUCAL | *Lucal* | in the North |
| 10.7 | AZIAZIOR | *aziázor* | in the likenes |
| 10.8 | PÆB | *pæb* | of an oke |
| 10.9 | SOBA | *Soba* | whose |
| 10.10 | LILONON | *Lilônon* | branches |
| 10.11 | CHIS | *chis* | are |
| 10.12 | VIRQ | *virq* | Nests |
| 10.13 | OP | *op* | 22 |
| 10.14 | EOPHAN | *eôphan* | of lamentation |
| 10.15 | OD | *od* | and |
| 10.16 | RACLIR | *raclir* | weaping |
| 10.17 | MAASI | *maâsi* | Layd up |
| 10.18 | BAGLE | *bagle* | for |
| 10.19 | CAOSGI | *caosgi* | the earth |
| 10.20 | DS | *ds* | which |
| 10.21 | IALPON | *ialpon* | burn |
| 10.22 | DOSIG | *dosig* | night |
| 10.23 | OD | *od* | and |

‡ 9.76 to 9.78: 'I' for 'is'; see 1.13, 4.50, &c. CORS for 'such'; see 2.36, 7.21, 30.144. TA for 'as'; see 1.14, 1.18, 1.27, 1.74, 2.15, &c.

| | | | |
|---|---|---|---|
| 10.24 | BASGIM | *basgim* | day: |
| 10.25 | OD | *od* | and |
| 10.26 | OXEX | *oxex* | vomit out |
| 10.27 | DAZIZ | *dazís* | the heds |
| 10.28 | SIATRIS | *siâtris* | of scorpions |
| 10.29 | OD | *od* | and |
| 10.30 | SALBROX | *salbrox* | live sulphur |
| 10.31 | CINXIR | *cynxir* | myngled |
| 10.32 | FABOAN | *fabôan* | with poyson |
| 10.33 | UNAL | *Vnâl-chis* | These |
| 10.34 | CHIS | | be‡ |
| 10.35 | CONST | *const* | The Thunders |
| 10.36 | DS | *ds* | that |
| 10.37 | DAOX | *dâox* | 5678 |
| 10.38 | COCASB | *cocasb* | tymes |
| 10.39 | OL | *ol* | in the 24th part |
| 10.40 | OANIO | *oánio* | of a moment |
| 10.41 | YOR | *yor* | rore |
| 10.42 | EORS | | with a hundred§ |
| 10.43 | MICAOLI | *vóhim* | mighty |
| 10.44 | OL | *ol* | |
| 10.45 | GIXYAX | *gizyax* | earthquakes |
| 10.46 | OD | *od* | and |
| 10.47 | MATB | *eórs* | a thousand |
| 10.48 | COCASB | *cocasg* | tymes* |
| 10.49 | PLOSI | *plosi* | as many |
| 10.50 | MOLUI | *molui* | surges |
| 10.51 | DS | *ds* | which |
| 10.52 | PAGEIP | *pagêip* | rest not |
| 10.53 | LARAG | *Larag* | neyther |
| 10.54 | OM | *om* | know |
| 10.55 | DROLN | *droln* | at any |

‡ 10.34: CHIS usually is 'are'.

§ 10.42 to 10.47: Large lacuna in Sl. MS. 3191. Dee put the English as marginalia. Dee experienced much confusion in this passage. See the July 5, 1584 working in Royal Appendix XLVI or *True Relation*. My reconstruction is only partial.

* 10.48: COCASB for 'times'; see 3.46, 9.75, 10.38, 10.57, 30.124.

| 10.56 | MATORB | *matorb*† | |
| 10.57 | COCASB | *cocasb* | tyme |
| 10.58 | EMNA | *emna* | here |
| 10.59 | L | *L* | One |
| 10.60 | PATRALX | *patralx* | rock |
| 10.61 | YOLCI | *yolci* | bringeth forth |
| 10.62 | MATB | *matb* | 1000 |
| 10.63 | NOMIG | *nomig* | even as |
| 10.64 | MONONS | *monons* | the hart |
| 10.65 | OLORA | *olôra* | of man |
| 10.66 | GNAY | *gnay* | doth |
| 10.67 | ANGELARD | *angêlard* | his thowghts |
| 10.68 | OHIO | *Ohîo* | wo |
| 10.69 | OHIO | *Ohîo* | wo |
| 10.70 | OHIO | *Ohîo* | wo |
| 10.71 | OHIO | *Ohîo* | wo |
| 10.72 | OHIO | *Ohîo* | wo |
| 10.73 | OHIO | *Ohîo* | wo |
| 10.74 | NOIB | *noib* | yea |
| 10.75 | OHIO | *Ohîo* | wo |
| 10.76 | CAOSGON | *Caósgon* | be to the earth |
| 10.77 | BAGLE | *Bagle* | For |
| 10.78 | MADRID | *madrid* | her iniquitie |
| 10.79 | I | *i* | is |
| 10.80 | ZIROP | *ziróp* | was |
| 10.81 | CHISO | *chiso* | and shal be |
| 10.82 | DRILPA | *drilpa* | great. |
| 10.83 | NIISO | *Niiso* | Come away |
| 10.84 | CRIP | *crip* | but |
| 10.85 | IP | *ip* | not |
| 10.86 | NIDALI | *nidâli* | your noyses. |

### THE ELEVENTH KEY

| 11.1 | OXIAYAL | *Oxiayal* | The mighty seat |
| 11.2 | HOLDO | *holdo* | groaned |

† 10.56: English missing in Sl. MS. 3191; Laycock gives MATORB as 'echoing'.

| | | | |
|---|---|---|---|
| 11.3 | OD | *od* | and |
| 11.4 | ZIROM | *zirom* | they were |
| 11.5 | O | O | :5: |
| 11.6 | CORAXO | *coráxo* | thunders |
| 11.7 | DS | *ds* | which |
| 11.8 | ZILDAR | *zildar* | flew |
| 11.9 | RAASY | *raâsy* | into the East |
| 11.10 | OD | *od* | and |
| 11.11 | VABZIR | *vabzir* | the Egle |
| 11.12 | CAMLIAX | *camlíax* | spake |
| 11.13 | OD | *od* | and |
| 11.14 | BAHAL | *báhal* | cryed with a lowde voyce |
| 11.15 | NIISO | *Niíso* | Come awaye |
| 11.16 | OD | | and† |
| 11.17 | ALDON | | they gathered them together in |
| 11.18 | SALMAN | *salman* | the house |
| 11.19 | TELOCH | *telóch* | of death |
| 11.20 | CASARMAN | *Ca-sár-man* | of whome |
| 11.21 | HOLQ | *hol-q* | it is measured |
| 11.22 | OD | *od* | and |
| 11.23 | T | *ti* | it |
| 11.24 | I | | is |
| 11.25 | TA | *ta* | as |
| 11.26 | ZCHIS | *z-chis* | they are |
| 11.27 | SOBA | *soba* | whose |
| 11.28 | CORMF | *cormf* | number |
| 11.29 | I | *i* | is |
| 11.30 | GA | *ga* | 31. |
| 11.31 | NIISO | *Niisa* | Come away |
| 11.32 | BAGLE | *Bagle* | For |
| 11.33 | ABRAMG | *abramg* | I have prepared |
| 11.34 | NONCP | *noncp* | for you |
| 11.35 | ZACAR | *ZACARe* | Move‡ |

† 11.16 to 11.17: Lacuna in Sl. MS. 3191. The Enochian is missing and the English is in the margin. Missing word probably has ALDO- stem; see 9.30, 17.21.

‡ 11.35: ZACARE possible alternate spelling for ZACAR? ZACAR appears 14 times in the opus; ZACARE twice; see 1.79.

| | | |
|---|---|---|
| 11.36 CA | *ca* | therfore |
| 11.37 OD | *od* | and |
| 11.38 ZAMRAN | *ZAMRAN* | shew your selves |
| 11.39 ODO | *odo* | open |
| 11.40 CICLE | *cicle* | the Mysteries |
| 11.41 QAA | *Qaá* | of your Creation |
| 11.42 ZORGE | *Zorge* | Be friendely unto me |
| 11.43 LAP | *lap* | for |
| 11.44 ZIRDO | *zirdo* | I am |
| 11.45 NOCO | *noco* | the servant |
| 11.46 MAD | *Mad* | of the same your God |
| 11.47 HOATH | *Hoath* | the true worshipper |
| 11.48 IAIDA | *Iaida.* | of the Highest. |

## THE TWELFTH KEY

| | | |
|---|---|---|
| 12.1 NONCI | *Nonci* | O you |
| 12.2 DS | *dsonf* | that |
| 12.3 SONF | | rayne§ |
| 12.4 BABAGE | *Babage* | in the sowth |
| 12.5 OD | *od* | and |
| 12.6 CHIS | *chis* | are |
| 12.7 OB | *ob* | :28: |
| 12.8 HUBARO | *hubíâo* | the lanterns* |
| 12.9 TIBIBP | *tibibp* | of sorrow |
| 12.10 ALLAR | *allar* | bynde up |
| 12.11 ATRAAH | *atraâh* | your girdles |
| 12.12 OD | *od* | and |
| 12.13 EF | *ef* | viset us |
| 12.14 DRIX | *drix* | Bring down |
| 12.15 FAFEN | *fafen* | your trayn |
| 12.16 MAIN | *Mian* | 3663 |
| 12.17 AR | *ar* | that |
| 12.18 ENAY | *Enay* | the Lord |
| 12.19 OVOF | *ovof* | may be magnified |
| 12.20 SOBA | *soba* | whose |

§ 12.3: SONF for 'which'; however, DSONF could be a contraction.
* 12.8: HUBAR- stem for 'lamp' or 'lantern'; see 5.39, 17.13.

| 12.21 | DOOAIN | *dooâin* | name |
| 12.22 | AAI | *aai* | amongst you |
| 12.23 | I | *i* | is |
| 12.24 | VONPH | *VONPH* | Wrath |
| 12.25 | ZACAR | *ZACAR* | Move, |
| 12.26 | GOHUS | *gohus* | I say, |
| 12.27 | OD | *od* | and |
| 12.28 | ZAMRAN | *ZAMRAN,* | shew yourselves |
| 12.29 | ODO | *odo* | open |
| 12.30 | CICLE | *cicle* | the mysteries |
| 12.31 | QAA | *Qáa,* | of your Creation |
| 12.32 | ZORGE | *Zorge,* | be friendly unto me |
| 12.33 | LAP | *Lap* | for |
| 12.34 | ZIRDO | *zirdo* | I am |
| 12.35 | NOCO | *noco* | the servant |
| 12.36 | MAD | *MAD* | of the same your God, |
| 12.37 | HOATH | *Hoath* | the true worshipper |
| 12.38 | IAIDA | *Iaida.* | of the Highest. |

### THE THIRTEENTH KEY

♊

| 13.1 | NAPEAI | *Napêai* | Oh you swords |
| 13.2 | BABAGEN | *Babâgen* | of the sowth |
| 13.3 | DS | *dsbrin* | which |
| 13.4 | BRIN | | have† |
| 13.5 | VX | *vx* | 42 |
| 13.6 | OOAONA | *ooáôna* | eyes |
| 13.7 | LRING | *lring* | to styr up |
| 13.8 | VONPH | *vonph* | wrath |
| 13.9 | DOALIM | *doâlim* | of synn |
| 13.10 | EOLIS | *eôlis* | making |
| 13.11 | OLLOG | *ollog* | men |
| 13.12 | ORSBA | *orsba* | drunken |
| 13.13 | DS | *ds* | which |
| 13.14 | CHIS | *chis* | are |
| 13.15 | AFFA | *affa* | empty: |

† 13.4: BRIN for 'have'; see 9.7, 14.6, 16.7, 17.11.

| 13.16 | MICMA | *Micma* | Behold |
| 13.17 | ISRO | *isro* | the promise |
| 13.18 | MAD | *MAD* | of God |
| 13.19 | OD | *od* | and |
| 13.20 | LONSHI | *Lon-shi -tox* | his powre |
| 13.21 | TOX† | | |
| 13.22 | DS | *ds* | which |
| 13.23 | IUMD | *ivmd* | is called |
| 13.24 | AAI | *aai* | amongst you |
| 13.25 | GROSB | *GROSB:* | A bitter sting: |
| 13.26 | ZACAR | *ZACAR* | Move |
| 13.27 | OD | *od* | and |
| 13.28 | ZAMRAN | *ZAMRAN,* | shew yourselves |
| 13.29 | ODO | *odo* | Open |
| 13.30 | CICLE | *cicle* | the mysteries |
| 13.31 | QAA | *Qäa,* | of your Creation |
| 13.32 | ZORGE | *Zorge,* | Be friendly unto me: |
| 13.33 | LAP | *Lap* | for |
| 13.34 | ZIRDO | *zirdo* | I am |
| 13.35 | NOCO | *Noco* | the servant |
| 13.36 | MAD | *MAD,* | of the same your God |
| 13.37 | HOATH | *Hoath* | The true worshipper |
| 13.38 | IAIDA | *Iaida.* | of the Highest |

### THE FOURTEENTH KEY

| 14.1 | NOROMI | *Norómi* | O you sonns |
| 14.2 | BAGIE | *bagíe* | of fury |
| 14.3 | PASBS | *pasbs* | the dowghters |
| 14.4 | OIAD | *oíad* | of the Just |
| 14.5 | DS | *ds* | which |
| 14.6 | TRINT | *trint* | sit |
| 14.7 | MIRC | *mirc* | uppon |
| 14.8 | OL | *ol* | 24 |
| 14.9 | THIL | *thil* | seats |
| 14.10 | DODS | *dods* | vexing |

† 13.21: Tox may be a suffix that expresses possession; see 14.23.

| 14.11 | TOL | *tolham* | all |
| 14.12 | HAMI | | creatures |
| 14.13 | CAOSGO | *caósgo* | of the earth |
| 14.14 | HOMIN | *Homin* | with age |
| 14.15 | DS | *ds* | which |
| 14.16 | BRIN | *brin* | have |
| 14.17 | OROCH | *oroch* | under you |
| 14.18 | QUAR | *Quar* | 1636 |
| 14.19 | MICMA | *Micma* | Behold |
| 14.20 | BIAL | *bial* | the voyce |
| 14.21 | OIAD | *oíad* | of God |
| 14.22 | AISRO | *aísro* | promys |
| 14.23 | TOX | *tox* | of him |
| 14.24 | DS | *dsivm* | which |
| 14.25 | IUMD | | is called‡ |
| 14.26 | AAI | *aai* | amongst you |
| 14.27 | BALTIM | *Baltim* | Furye, or Extreme Justice |
| 14.28 | ZACAR | *ZACAR* | Move |
| 14.29 | OD | *od* | and |
| 14.30 | ZAMRAN | *ZAMRAN* | shew yourselves |
| 14.31 | ODO | *odo* | open |
| 14.32 | CICLE | *cicle* | the mysteries |
| 14.33 | QAA | *Qãa,* | of your Creation |
| 14.34 | ZORGE | *Zorge,* | Be friendly unto me |
| 14.35 | LAP | *Lap* | for |
| 14.36 | ZIRDO | *zirdo* | I am |
| 14.37 | NOCO | *Noco* | the servant |
| 14.38 | MAD | *MAD,* | of the same your God |
| 14.39 | HOATH | *hoath* | the true worshipper |
| 14.40 | IAIDA | *Iaída.* | of the Highest. |

### THE FIFTEENTH KEY

☿

| 15.1 | ILS | *Ils* | O thow |
| 15.2 | TABAAM | *tabâan* | the governor |
| 15.3 | L | *Liálprt* | of the first |

‡ 14.25: IUMD for 'is called'; see 13.23, 18.19.

| 15.4 | IALPRT | | flame‡ |
| 15.5 | CASARMAN | *casarman* | under whose |
| 15.6 | UPAAH | *vpaáhi* | wyngs |
| 15.7 | CHIS | *chis* | are |
| 15.8 | DARG | *darg* | 6739 |
| 15.9 | DS | *dsoâdo* | which |
| 15.10 | OADO | | weave |
| 15.11 | CAOSGI | *caôsgi* | the earth |
| 15.12 | ORSCOR | *orscor* | with drynes |
| 15.13 | DS | *ds* | which |
| 15.14 | OMAX | *ômax* | knowest |
| 15.15 | MONASCI | *monasci* | of the great name |
| 15.16 | BÆOVIB | *Bæôuib* | Righteousnes§ |
| 15.17 | OD | *od* | and |
| 15.18 | EMETGIS | *emetgis* | the seale |
| 15.19 | IAIADIX | *iaiâdix* | of Honor |
| 15.20 | ZACAR | *ZACAR* | Move |
| 15.21 | OD | *od* | and |
| 15.22 | ZAMRAN | *ZAMRAN,* | shew yourselves |
| 15.23 | ODO | *odo* | open |
| 15.24 | CICLE | *cicle* | the mysteries |
| 15.25 | QAA | *Qäa* | of your Creation |
| 15.26 | ZORGE | *zorge,* | Be friendly unto me |
| 15.27 | LAP | *Lap* | for |
| 15.28 | ZIRDO | *zirdo* | I am |
| 15.29 | NOCO | *Noco* | the servant |
| 15.30 | MAD | *MAD,* | of the same your God |
| 15.31 | HOATH | *hoath* | the true worshipper |
| 15.32 | IAIDA | *Iaida.* | of the Highest. |

THE SIXTEENTH KEY

♈

| 16.1 | ILS | *Ils* | Oh thow |
| 16.2 | VIV | *viuîâlprt* | second |
| 16.3 | IALPRT | | flame |

‡ 15.4: IALPRT for 'flame'; see 16.3, 17.3; IALPRT only appears in contraction forms, but see also 18.5 & 2.10; IALPRG for 'burning flame'.

§ 15.16: Why not BALTOH for 'righteousness'? (See 1.76, 2.23, 9.67.) Could *Bæouib* be a proper noun?

| 16.4 | SALMAN | *salman* | the house |
| 16.5 | BALT | *balt* | of Justice |
| 16.6 | DS | *ds* | which |
| 16.7 | BRIN | | hast |
| 16.8 | ACROODZI | *acroódzi* | thy beginning |
| 16.9 | BUSD | *busd* | in glory: |
| 16.10 | OD | *od* | and |
| 16.11 | BLIORAX | *bliôrax* | shalt comfort |
| 16.12 | BALIT | *balit* | the iust: |
| 16.13 | DS | *dsinsi* | which |
| 16.14 | INSI | | walkest |
| 16.15 | CAOSG | *caosg* | on the earth |
| 16.16 | LUSDAN | *lusdan* | with feete |
| 16.17 | EMOD | *Emod* | 876 |
| 16.18 | DS | *dsom* | that |
| 16.19 | OM | | understand* |
| 16.20 | OD | *od* | and |
| 16.21 | TLIOB | *tliob* | separate |
| 16.22 | HAMI | | creatures:† |
| 16.23 | DRILPA | *drilpa* | great |
| 16.24 | GEH | *geh* | art |
| 16.25 | ILS | *yls* | thow |
| 16.26 | MADZILODARP | | |
| | | *Madzilodarp* | in the God of stretch-forth-and-conquer. |
| 16.27 | ZACAR | *ZACAR* | Move |
| 16.28 | OD | *od* | and |
| 16.29 | ZAMRAN | *ZAMRAN* | shew yourselves |
| 16.30 | ODO | *odo* | Open |
| 16.31 | CICLB | *cicle* | the mysteries |
| 16.32 | QAA | *Qāa* | of your Creation |
| 16.33 | ZORGE | *zorge,* | Be friendely unto me |
| 16.34 | LAP | *Lap* | for |
| 16.35 | ZIRDO | *zirdo* | I am |
| 16.36 | NOCO | *Noco* | the servant |
| 16.37 | MAD | *Mad* | of the same your God |

\* 16.19: OM for 'understand' or 'know'; see 2.4, 10.54, 30.113.

† 16.22: HAM- stem for 'creatures'; see 7.25, 14.12.

| 16.38 | HOATH | *hoath* | the true worshipper |
| 16.39 | IAIDA | *Iaída.* | of the Highest. |

### THE SEVENTEENTH KEY

☿

| 17.1 | ILS | *Ils* | O thow |
| 17.2 | D | *dialprt* | third |
| 17.3 | IALPRT | | flame |
| 17.4 | SOBA | *soba* | whose |
| 17.5 | UPAAH | *vpâah* | wyngs |
| 17.6 | CHIS | *chis* | are |
| 17.7 | NANBA | *nanba* | thorns |
| 17.8 | ZIXLAY | *zixlay* | to styr up |
| 17.9 | DODSIH | *dodsih* | vexation: |
| 17.10 | OD | *od* | and |
| 17.11 | BRIN | *brint* | hast |
| 17.12 | FAXS | *Faxs* | 7336 |
| 17.13 | HUBARO | *hubâro* | lamps living |
| 17.14 | TUSTAX | *tustax* | going |
| 17.15 | YLSI | *ylsi,* | before the |
| 17.16 | SOBA | *sobaíad* | whose |
| 17.17 | IAD | | God |
| 17.18 | I | *i* | is |
| 17.19 | VONPOVNPH | *vónpôvnph* | Wrath in Angre* |
| 17.20 | ALDON | *Aldon* | Gyrd up |
| 17.21 | DAXIL | *daxil* | thy loynes |
| 17.22 | OD | *od* | and |
| 17.23 | TOATAR | *toátar:* | harken |
| 17.24 | ZACAR | *ZACAR* | Move |
| 17.25 | OD | *od* | and |
| 17.26 | ZAMRAN | *ZAMRAN* | shew yourselves |
| 17.27 | ODO | *odo* | Open |
| 17.28 | CICLE | *cicle* | the mysteries |
| 17.29 | QAA | *Qäa,* | of your Creation |
| 17.30 | ZORGE | *zorge,* | Be friendly unto me |

\* 17.19: Contraction of VONPHO–VONPH or 'of wrath'-'wrath'. This appears to be a peculiar kind of emphatic redundancy.

| 17.31 | LAP | *Lap* | for |
| 17.32 | ZIRDO | *zirdo* | I am |
| 17.33 | NOCO | *Noco* | the servant |
| 17.34 | MAD | *Mad* | of the same your God |
| 17.35 | HOATH | *hoath* | the true worshipper |
| 17.36 | IAIDA | *Iaïda* | of the Highest. |

THE EIGHTEENTH KEY

☋

| 18.1 | ILS | *Ils* | O thow |
| 18.2 | MICAOLZ | *Micaólz* | mighty |
| 18.3 | OLPIRT | *Olprit* | light |
| 18.4 | OD | | and |
| 18.5 | IALPRG | *ialprg* | burning flame |
| 18.6 | BLIORS | *Bliors* | of comfort |
| 18.7 | DS | *ds* | which |
| 18.8 | ODO | *odo* | openest |
| 18.9 | BUSDIR | *Busdir* | the glory |
| 18.10 | OIAD | *oîad* | of God |
| 18.11 | OVOARS | *ouðars* | to the center |
| 18.12 | CAOSGO | *caósgo* | of the erth |
| 18.13 | CASARMG | *Casarmg* | In whome |
| 18.14 | LAIAD | *Laíad* | the secrets of truth |
| 18.15 | ERAN | *erán* | 6332 |
| 18.16 | BRINTS | *brints* | have |
| 18.17 | CASASAM | *casâsam* | their abiding |
| 18.18 | DS | *ds* | which |
| 18.19 | IUMD | *ivmd* | is called |
| 18.20 | ACLONDOH | *á-q-lo adóhi* | in thy Kingdome |
| 18.21 | MOZ | *MOZ* | IOYE |
| 18.22 | OD | *od* | and |
| 18.23 | MAOFFAS | *maóffas* | not to be measured |
| 18.24 | BOLP | *Bolp* | Be thow |
| 18.25 | COMO | *comobliort* | a wyndow |
| 18.26 | BLIORT | | of comfort |
| 18.27 | PAMBT | *pambt* | vnto me. |
| 18.28 | ZACAR | *ZACAR* | Move |
| 18.29 | OD | *od* | and |

| 18.30 | ZAMRAN | *ZAMRAN* | shew yourselves |
| 18.31 | ODO | *odo* | Open |
| 18.32 | CICLE | *cicle* | the mysteries |
| 18.33 | QAA | *Qäa,* | of your Creation |
| 18.34 | ZORGE | *zorge* | Be friendely unto me |
| 18.35 | LAP | *Lap* | for |
| 18.36 | ZIRDO | *zirdo* | I am |
| 18.37 | NOCO | *Noco* | the servant |
| 18.38 | MAD | *MAD* | of the same your God |
| 18.39 | HOATH | *Hoath* | the true worshipper |
| 18.40 | IAIDA | *Iaïda.* | of the Highest. |

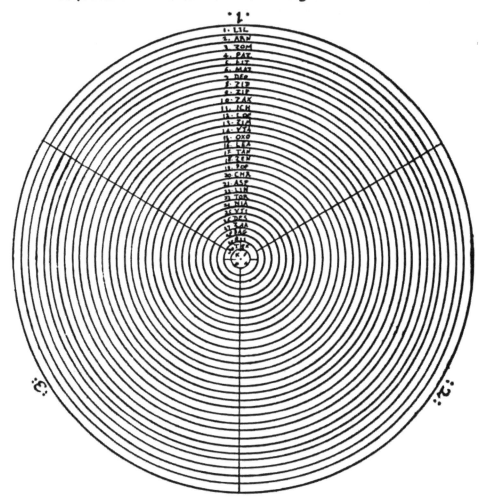

## THE KEY OF THE THIRTY AYRES

♃

| | | | |
|---|---|---|---|
| 30.1 | MADRIAX | *Madríax* | Oh you hevens |
| 30.2 | DS | *dspraf* | which |
| 30.3 | PRAF | | dwell |
| 30.4 | LIL | *LIL* | in the first Ayre, [⁑] |
| 30.5 | CHIS | *chis* | are |
| 30.6 | MICAOLZ | *Micaólz* | Mightie |
| 30.7 | SAANIR | *saánir* | in the partes |
| 30.8 | CAOSGO | *Caósgo* | of the Erth, |
| 30.9 | OD | *od* | and |
| 30.10 | FISIS | *físis* | execute |
| 30.11 | BALZIZRAS | *balzizras* | the Judgement |
| 30.12 | IAIDA | *Iaída* | of the highest |
| 30.13 | NONCA | *nonca* | to you |
| 30.14 | GOHULIM | *gohúlim* | it is sayd, |
| 30.15 | MICMA | *Micma* | Beholde |
| 30.16 | ADOIAN | *adoían* | the face |
| 30.17 | MAD | *MAD* | of your God, |
| 30.18 | IAOD | *Jáod* | the begynning |
| 30.19 | BLIORB | *bliorb* | of comfort: |
| 30.20 | SOBA | *sabaoodôna* | whose |
| 30.21 | OOAONA | | eyes§ |
| 30.22 | CHIS | *chis* | are |
| 30.23 | LUCIFTIAS | *Lucíftías* | the brightnes |
| 30.24 | PERIPSOL | *perípsol* | of the hevens: |
| 30.25 | DS | *ds* | which |
| 30.26 | ABRAASSA | *abraássa* | provided |
| 30.27 | NONCF | *noncf* | you |
| 30.28 | NETAAIB | *netââib* | for the government |
| 30.29 | CAOSGO | *Caósgi* | of the Erth.* |
| 30.30 | OD | *od* | and |

⁑ The name of the ayre being invoked is inserted here. The ayres are listed in the margin of Sl. MS. 3191 as well as on the preceeding figure. A more detailed description of the ayres and the beings attributed to each ayre is given in Book Four of this volume.

§ 30.21: OOAONA for 'eyes'; see 13.6.

* 30.29: CAOSGO for 'of the earth'; see 8.35, 8.63, 9.32, 14.13, 30.8. CAOSGI is 'the earth'; see 4.44, 5.26.

☞DIAGRAM OF THE 30 AYRES]

G

| | | | |
|---|---|---|---|
| 30.31 | TILB | *tilb* | her |
| 30.32 | ADPHAHT | *adphaht* | unspeakable |
| 30.33 | DAMPLOZ | *dámploz* | varietie |
| 30.34 | TOOAT | *toóat* | furnishing |
| 30.35 | NONCF | *noncf* | you |
| 30.36 | GMICALZ | *gmicálzôma* | with a powr |
| 30.37 | OM | | understanding* |
| 30.38 | LRASD | *Lrásd* | to dispose |
| 30.39 | TOFGLO | *tófglo* | all things |
| 30.40 | MARB | *marb* | according |
| 30.41 | YARRY | *yárry* | to the providence |
| 30.42 | IDOIGO | *IDOIGO* | of him that sitteth on the holy Throne |
| 30.43 | OD | *od* | and |
| 30.44 | TORZULP | *torzulp* | rose up |
| 30.45 | IAODAF | *idodaf* | in the begynning |
| 30.46 | GOHOL | *gohól* | saying, |
| 30.47 | CAOSGI | *Caósga* | The Earth |
| 30.48 | TABAORD | *tabaord* | Let her be governed |
| 30.49 | SAANIR | *saánir* | by her parts |
| 30.50 | OD | *od* | and |
| 30.51 | CHRISTEOS | *christéós* | Let there be |
| 30.52 | YRPOIL | *yrpóil* | Division |
| 30.53 | TIOBL | *tióbl* | in her, |
| 30.54 | BUSDIR | *Busdir* | that the glory |
| 30.55 | TILB | *tilb* | of hir |
| 30.56 | NOALN | *noaln* | may be |
| 30.57 | PAID | *paid* | allwayes |
| 30.58 | ORSBA | *orsba* | drunken |
| 30.59 | OD | *od* | and |
| 30.60 | DODRMNI | *dodrmni* | vexed |
| 30.61 | ZYLNA | *zylna* | in itself: |
| 30.62 | ELZAP | *Elzáptilb* | Her course, |
| 30.63 | TILB‡ | | |

* 30.37: OM for 'understanding'; see 2.4, 10.54, 16.19.
‡ 30.63: TILB for 'of her'; see 30.55. Could TILB be another suffix (like TOX) signifying possession?

| 30.64 | PARMGI | *parmgi* | let it ronne |
| 30.65 | PERIPSAX | *perípsax* | with the hevens: |
| 30.66 | OD | *od* | and |
| 30.67 | TA | *ta* | as |
| 30.68 | QURLST | *qurlst* | a handmayd |
| 30.69 | BOOAPIS | *booapiS* | let her serve them: |
| 30.70 | L | *Lnibm* | One |
| 30.71 | NIMB | | season |
| 30.72 | OUCHO | *ovcho* | Let it confownd |
| 30.73 | SYMP | *symp,* | another: |
| 30.74 | OD | *od* | And |
| 30.75 | CHRISTEOS | *Christéos* | let there be |
| 30.76 | AG | *Agtoltorn* | no |
| 30.77 | TOLTORN | | Creature‡ |
| 30.78 | MIRC | *mirc* | uppon |
| 30.79 | Q | *Q* | or |
| 30.80 | TIOBL | *tióbl* | within her |
| 30.81 | LEL | *Lel,* | the same: |
| 30.82 | TOL | *Ton* | All |
| 30.83 | PAOMBD | *paombd* | her members |
| 30.84 | DILZMO | *dilzmo* | let them differ |
| 30.85 | ASPIAN | *aspian,* | in their qualities: |
| 30.86 | OD | *Od* | And |
| 30.87 | CHRISTEOS | *christêos* | let there be |
| 30.88 | AG | *ag* | no |
| 30.89 | L | *L* | one |
| 30.90 | TOLTORN | *tortorn* | Creature |
| 30.91 | PARACH | *parach* | æquall |
| 30.92 | ASYMP | *asymp,* | with another |
| 30.93 | CORDZIZ | *Cordziz* | The reasonable Creatures of Erth or Men |
| 30.94 | DODPAL | *dodpal* | let them vex |
| 30.95 | OD | *od* | and |
| 30.96 | FIFALZ | *fifalz* | weede out |
| 30.97 | L | *Lsmnad,* | one |
| 30.98 | SMNAD | | another: |

‡ 30.77: TOLTORN for 'creatures'; see 30.90.

GG

| | | |
|---|---|---|
| 30.99 OD | *od* | And |
| 30.100 FARGT | *fargt* | the dwelling places, |
| 30.101 BAMS | *bams* | let them forget |
| 30.102 OMAOAS | *omaóas,* | their names: |
| 30.103 CONISBRA | *Conísbra* | The work of man |
| 30.104 OD | *od* | and |
| 30.105 AVAVOX | *auåuox* | his pomp, |
| 30.106 TONUG | *tcnug,* | let them be defaced: |
| 30.107 ORSCA | *Orscatbl* | His buyldings |
| 30.108 TLB | | |
| 30.109 NOASMI | *noåsmi* | let them become |
| 30.110 TABGES | *tabges,* | Caves |
| 30.111 LEVITHMONG | *Levithmong* | for the beasts of the feild: |
| 30.112 UNCHI | *unchi* | Confownd |
| 30.113 OM | *omptilb* | her understanding |
| 30.114 TILB‡ | | |
| 30.115 ORS | *ors.* | with darknes. |
| 30.116 BAGLE | *Bagle* | For why? |
| 30.117 MOOOAH | *Moóåh* | It repenteth me |
| 30.118 OL | *ɔlcórdziz.* | I made§ |
| 30.119 CORDZIZ | | Man. |
| 30.120 L | *L* | One |
| 30.121 CAPIMAO | *capîmao* | while |
| 30.122 IXOMAXIP | *ixomaxip* | let her be known, |
| 30.123 OD | *od* | and |
| 30.124 CA | *cacócasb* | another |
| 30.125 CAPIMAO | | while‡ |
| 30.126 GOSAA | *gosåa.* | a stranger: |
| 30.127 BAGLEN | *Baglen* | Bycause |
| 30.128 PI | *pii* | she |
| 30.129 I | | is |
| 30.130 TIANTA | *tianta* | the bed |
| 30.131 ABABALOND | *abábâlond* | of an Harlot, |

‡ 30.114: The English would be better rendered as 'the understanding of her'; see note on 30.63.

§ 30.118: Possibly a contraction—if so, a word is missing. OL is 'I' (first person singular), while CORDZIZ is 'men'. Perhaps the 'made' is somehow understood?

‡ 30.125: The English probably should be 'time'; see 4.32.

| | | | |
|---|---|---|---|
| 30.132 | OD | *od* | and |
| 30.133 | FAORGT | *faórgt* | the dwelling place |
| 30.134 | TELOCVOVIM | *telocvovim.* | of him that is faln:* |
| 30.135 | MADRIIAX | *Mádríiax* | O you hevens, |
| 30.136 | TORZU | *torzu* | arrise, |
| 30.137 | OADRIAX | *oádriax* | the lower hevens |
| 30.138 | OROCHA | *orócha* | underneath you, |
| 30.139 | ABOAPRI | *abóápri.* | Let them serve you: |
| 30.140 | TABAORI | *Tabáóri* | Govern |
| 30.141 | PRIAZ | *priáz* | those |
| 30.142 | AR | *artabas.* | that† |
| 30.143 | TABAORI | | govern: |
| 30.144 | ADRPAN | *Adrpan* | Cast down |
| 30.144 | ADRPAN | | Cast down |
| 30.145 | CORS | *corsta* | such |
| 30.146 | TA | | as |
| 30.147 | DOBIX | *dobix.* | fall: |
| 30.148 | YOLCAM | *Yolcam* | Bring forth |
| 30.149 | PRIAZI | *priazi* | with those |
| 30.150 | AR | *arcoazior.* | that |
| 30.151 | COAZIOR | | encrease: |
| 30.152 | OD | *od ♥* | And |
| 30.153 | QUASB | *quasb* | destroy |
| 30.154 | QTING | *qting.* | the rotten: |
| 30.155 | RIPIR | *Ripír* | No place |
| 30.156 | PAAOXT | *paaoxt* | let it remayne |
| 30.157 | SAGACOR | *sagácor.* | in one number: |
| 30.158 | UML | *vml* | Ad |
| 30.159 | OD | *od* | and |
| 30.160 | PRDZAR | *prd-zar* | Diminish |
| 30.161 | CACRG | *cácrg* | vntill |
| 30.162 | AOIVEÆ | *Aoivéâe* | the stars |
| 30.163 | CORMPT | *cormpt.* | be numbred: |
| 30.164 | TORZU | *TORZU* | ARRISE, |

* 30.134: Contraction of TELOCH-VOVIN or 'death'-'dragon'. In this case the fallen one is the great dragon Coronzon..

† 30.142 to 30.143: AR for 'that'; see 12.17; TABAORI for 'govern'; see 30.140.

| | | |
|---|---|---|
| 30.165 ZACAR | *ZACAR* | MOVE, |
| 30.166 OD | *od* | and |
| 30.167 ZAMRAN | *ZAMRAN* | APPERE |
| 30.168 ASPT | *aspt* | before |
| 30.169 SIBSI | *sibsi* | the Covenant |
| 30.170 BUTMONA | *butmôna* | of his mowth, |
| 30.171 DS | *ds* | which |
| 30.172 SURZAS | *surzas* | he hath sworne |
| 30.173 TIA | *tia* | unto us |
| 30.174 BALTAN | *baltan:* | in his Justice: |
| 30.175 ODO | *Odo* | OPEN |
| 30.176 CICLE | *cicle* | the Mysteries |
| 30.177 QAA | *Qáa:* | of your Creation: |
| 30.178 OD | *od* | And |
| 30.179 OZAZMA | *ozazma* | Make us |
| 30.180 PLAPLI | *plapli* | partakers |
| 30.181 IADNAMAD | *Iadnâmad* | of undefyled knowledg.‡ |

‡ 30.181: Contraction IAD–NAMAD or 'God'-'knowledge'.

# BOOK FOUR
# EARTHLY KNOWLEDGE, AID & VICTORY

🐚

HEN THE MOST HIGH DIVIDED TO THE NATIONS THEIR inheritance, when he separated the sons of Adam, he set the bounds of the people according to the number of the children of Isræl\*. ⸭And had a wall great and high, and had twelve gates, and at the gates twelve angels, and names written thereon, which are the names of the twelve tribes of the children of Isræl†.

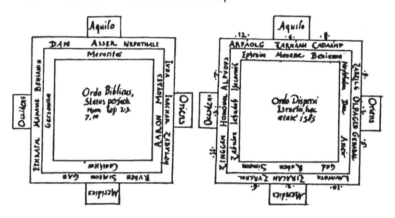

\* *Deuteronomy,* Chapter 32.    † *Revelation,* Chapter 21.

[*NB.* The following captions are to be read for the numbered columns following:—ED.]

1.] Part of the Earth as imposed by Man.
2.] Part of the Earth as imposed by God.
3.] Divinely ordained Symetric Characters.
4.] Ordered Sphere of good & noble Ayres.
5.] Number of Good Ministers ordered in 3 parts.
6.] Total of all good Ministers.
7.] Angelic Kings Ruling the 30 orders and also the 12 tribes.
8.] Tribes of the people of Isræl Dispersed.
9.] Quarter of the Earth to which the dispersed tribes are assigned.

| O | 1 | 2 | 3 | 4 | 5 |
|---|---|---|---|---|---|
| 1. | Ægyptus | Occodon | | | 7209 |
| 2. | Syria | Pascomb | | Order 1: LIL | 2360 |
| 3. | Mesopotamia | Valgars | | | 5362 |
| 4. | Cappadocia | Doagnis | | | 3636 |
| 5. | Tuscia | Pacasna | | Order 2: ARN | 2362 |
| 6. | Asia Minor | Dialioai | | | 8962 |
| 7. | Hyrcaina | Samapha | | | 4400 |
| 8. | Thracia | Virooli | | Order 3: ZOM | 3660 |
| 9. | Gosmam | Andispi | | | 9236 |
| 10. | Thebaidi | Thotanp | | | 2360 |
| 11. | Parsadal | Axziarg | | Order 4: PAZ | 3000 |
| 12. | India | Pothnir | | | 6300 |
| 13. | Bactriane | Lazdixi | | | 8630 |
| 14. | Cilicia | Nocamal | | Order 5: LIT | 2306 |
| 15. | Oxiana | Tiarpax | | | 5802 |

| 0 | 6 | 7 | | 8 | 9 |
|---|---|---|---|---|---|
| 1. | | ZARZILG | 9 | Nephthalim | East N-E |
| 2. | 14931 | ZINGGEN | 11 | Zabulon | West S-W |
| 3. | | ALPUDUS | 7 | Isacaraah | West N-W |
| 4. | | ZARNAAH | 4 | Manasse | North |
| 5. | 15960 | ZIRACAH | 2 | Ruben | South |
| 6. | | ZIRACAH | 2 | Ruben | South |
| 7. | | ZARZILG | 9 | Nephthalim | East N-E |
| 8. | 17296 | ALPUDUS | 7 | Isacaraah | West N-W |
| 9. | | LAVAVOTH | 10 | Gad | South S-E |
| 10. | | LAVAVOTH | 10 | Gad | South S-E |
| 11. | 11660 | LAVAVOTH | 10 | Gad | South S-E |
| 12. | | ARFAOLG | 12 | Ephraim | North N-W |
| 13. | | OLPAGED | 1 | Dan | East |
| 14. | 16738 | ALPUDUS | 7 | Isacaraah | West N-W |
| 15. | | ZINGGEN | 11 | Zabulon | West S-W |

| 0 | 1 | 2 | 3 | 4 | 5 |
|---|---|---|---|---|---|
| 16. | Numidia | Saxtomp | | | 3620 |
| 17. | Cyprus | Vavaamp | | Order 6: MAZ | 9200 |
| 18. | Parthia | Zirzird | | | 7220 |
| 19. | Getulia | Opmacas | | | 6363 |
| 20. | Arabia | Genadol | | Order 7: DEO | 7706 |
| 21. | Phalagon | Aspiaon | | | 6320 |
| 22. | Mantiana | Zamfres | | | 4362 |
| 23. | Soxia | Todnaon | | Order 8: ZID | 7236 |
| 24. | Gallia | Pristac | | | 2302 |
| 25. | Assyria | Oddiorg | | | 9996 |
| 26. | Sogdiana | Cralpir | | Order 9: ZIP | 3620 |
| 27. | Lydia | Doanzin | | | 4230 |
| 28. | Caspis | Lexarph | | | 8880 |
| 29. | Germania | Comanan | | Order 10: ZAX | 1230 |
| 30. | Trenam | Tabitom | | | 1617 |

| 0 | 6 | 7 | | 8 | 9 |
|---|---|---|---|---|---|
| 16. | | GEBABAL | 5 | Asseir | East S-E |
| 17. | 20040 | ARFAOLG | 12 | Ephraim | North N-W |
| 18. | | GEBABAL | 5 | Asseir | East S-E |
| 19. | | ZARNAAH | 4 | Manasse | North |
| 20. | 20389 | HONONOL | 3 | Iehudah | West |
| 21. | | ZINGGEN | 11 | Zabulon | West S-W |
| 22. | | GEBABAL | 5 | Asseir | East S-E |
| 23. | 13900 | OLPAGED | 1 | Dan | East |
| 24. | | ZARZILG | 9 | Nephthalim | East N-E |
| 25. | | HONONOL | 3 | Iehudah | West |
| 26. | 17846 | LAVAVOTH | 10 | Gad | South S-E |
| 27. | | ZARZILG | 9 | Nephthalim | East N-E |
| 28. | | ZINGGEN | 11 | Zabulon | West S-W |
| 29. | 11727 | ALPUDUS | 7 | Isacaraah | West N-W |
| 30. | | ZARZILG | 9 | Nephthalim | East N-E |

| O | I | 2 | 3 | 4 | 5 |
|---|---|---|---|---|---|
| 31. | Bithynia | Molpand | | | 3472 |
| 32. | Gracia | Usnarda | | Order 11: ICH | 7236 |
| 33. | Lacia | Ponodol | | | 5234 |
| 34. | Onigap | Tapamal | | | 2658 |
| 35. | India Major | Gedoons | | Order 12: LOE | 7772 |
| 36. | Orchenij | Ambriol | | | 3391 |
| 37. | Achaia | Gecaond | | | 8111 |
| 38. | Armenia | Laparin | | Order 13: ZIM | 3360 |
| 39. | Nemrodiana | Docepax | | | 4213 |
| 40. | Paphlogonia | Tedoond | | | 2673 |
| 41. | Phasiana | Vivipos | | Order 14: UTA | 9236 |
| 42. | Chaldei | Ooanamb | | | 8230 |
| 43. | Itergi | Tahamdo | | | 1367 |
| 44. | Macedonia | Nociabi | | Order 15: OXO | 1367 |
| 45. | Garamannia | Tastoxo | | | 1886 |

| 0 | 6 | 7 | | 8 | 9 |
|---|---|---|---|---|---|
| 31. | | LAVAVOTH | 10 | Gad | South S-E |
| 32. | 15942 | ZURCHOL | 6 | Simeon | South S-W |
| 33. | | HONONOL | 3 | Iehudah | West |
| 34. | | ZURCHOL | 6 | Simeon | South S-W |
| 35. | 13821 | CADAAMP | 8 | Benjamin | North N-E |
| 36. | | ZIRACAH | 2 | Ruben | South |
| 37. | | LAVAVOTH | 10 | Gad | South S-E |
| 38. | 15684 | OLPAGED | 1 | Dan | East |
| 39. | | ALPUDUS | 7 | Isacaraah | West N-W |
| 40. | | GEBABAL | 5 | Asseir | East S-E |
| 41. | 20139 | ALPUDUS | 7 | Isacaraah | West N-W |
| 42. | | ARFAOLG | 12 | Ephraim | North N-W |
| 43. | | ZARZILG | 9 | Nephthalim | East N-E |
| 44. | 4620 | LAVAVOTH | 10 | Gad | South S-E |
| 45. | | ARFAOLG | 12 | Ephraim | North N-W |

| 0 | 1 | 2 | 3 | 4 | 5 |
|---|---|---|---|---|---|
| 46. | Sauromatica | Cucarpt | | | 9920 |
| 47. | Æthiopia | Lauacon | | Order 16: LEA | 9230 |
| 48. | Fiacim | Sochial | | | 9240 |
| 49. | Colchica | Sigmorf | | | 7623 |
| 50. | Cireniaca | Avdropt | | Order 17: TAN | 7132 |
| 51. | Nasamoma | Tocarzi | | | 2634 |
| 52. | Carthago | Nabaomi | | | 2346 |
| 53. | Coxlant | Zafasai | | Order 18: ZEN | 7689 |
| 54. | Adumea | Yalpamb | | | 9276 |
| 55. | Parstavia | Torzoxi | | | 6236 |
| 56. | Celtica | Abriond | | Order 19: POP | 6732 |
| 57. | Vinsan | Omagrap | | | 2388 |
| 58. | Tolpam | Zildron | | | 3626 |
| 59. | Carcedoma | Parziba | | Order 20: CHR | 7629 |
| 60. | Italia | Totocan | | | 3634 |

| 0 | 6 | 7 | | 8 | 9 |
|---|---|---|---|---|---|
| 46. | | ZIRACAH | 2 | Ruben | South |
| 47. | 28390 | HONONOL | 3 | Iehudah | West |
| 48. | | ARFAOLG | 12 | Ephraim | North N-W |
| 49. | | ZIRACAH | 2 | Ruben | South |
| 50. | 17389 | OLPAGED | 1 | Dan | East |
| 51. | | ZARZILG | 9 | Nephthalim | East N-E |
| 52. | | GEBABAL | 5 | Asseir | East S-E |
| 53. | 19311 | ALPUDUS | 7 | Isacaraah | West N-W |
| 54. | | ARFAOLG | 12 | Ephraim | North N-W |
| 55. | | ARFAOLG | 12 | Ephraim | North N-W |
| 56. | 15356 | CADAAMP | 8 | Benjamin | North N-E |
| 57. | | ZINGGEN | 11 | Zabulon | West S-W |
| 58. | | GEBABAL | 5 | Asseir | East S-E |
| 59. | 14889 | HONONOL | 3 | Iehudah | West |
| 60. | | ALPUDUS | 7 | Isacaraah | West N-W |

| 0 | 1 | 2 | 3 | 4 | 5 |
|---|---|---|---|---|---|
| 61. | Brytania | Chirzpa | | Order 21: ASP | 5536 |
| 62. | Phenices | Toantom | | | 5635 |
| 63. | Comaginen | Vixpalg | | | 5658 |
| 64. | Apulia | Ozidaia | | Order 22: LIN | 2232 |
| 65. | Marmarica | Paraoan | | | 2326 |
| 66. | Concava Syria | Calzirg | | | 2367 |
| 67. | Gebal | Ronoomb | | Order 23: TOR | 7320 |
| 68. | Elam | Onizimp | | | 7262 |
| 69. | Adunia | Zaxanin | | | 7333 |
| 70. | Media | Orcanir | | Order 24: NIA | 8200 |
| 71. | Arriana | Chialps | | | 8360 |
| 72. | Chaldea | Soageel | | | 8236 |
| 73. | Serica Populi | Mirzind | | Order 25: UTI | 5632 |
| 74. | Persia | Obvaors | | | 6333 |
| 75. | Gongatha | Ranglam | | | 6236 |

| 0 | 6 | 7 | | 8 | 9 |
|---|---|---|---|---|---|
| 61. | | ARFAOLG | 12 | Ephraim | North N-W |
| 62. | 16829 | CADAAMP | 8 | Benjamin | North N-E |
| 63. | | ZURCHOL | 6 | Simeon | South S-W |
| 64. | | ARFAOLG | 12 | Ephraim | North N-W |
| 65. | 6925 | OLPAGED | 1 | Dan | East |
| 66. | | ARFAOLG | 12 | Ephraim | North N-W |
| 67. | | ZARNAAH | 4 | Manasse | North |
| 68. | 21915 | LAVAVOTH | 10 | Gad | South S-E |
| 69. | | ZINGGEN | 11 | Zabulon | West S-W |
| 70. | | ZARNAAH | 4 | Manasse | North |
| 71. | 24796 | LAVAVOTH | 10 | Gad | South S-E |
| 72. | | ZINGGEN | 11 | Zabulon | West S-W |
| 73. | | ZARNAAH | 4 | Manasse | North |
| 74. | 18201 | ZIRACAH | 2 | Ruben | South |
| 75. | | ARFAOLG | 12 | Ephraim | North N-W |

H

| 0 | 1 | 2 | 3 | 4 | 5 |
|---|---|---|---|---|---|
| 76. | Gorsin | Pophand | | | 9232 |
| 77. | Hispania | Nigrana | | Order 26: DES | 3620 |
| 78. | Pamphilia | Bazchim | | | 5637 |
| 79. | Oacidi | Saziami | | | 7220 |
| 80. | Babylon | Mathula | | Order 27: ZAA | 7560 |
| 81. | Median | Orpanib | | | 7263 |
| 82. | Adumian | Labnixp | | | 2630 |
| 83. | Fœlix Arabia | Pocisni | | Order 28: BAG | 7236 |
| 84. | Metagoniti-dim | Oxlopar | | | 8200 |
| 85. | Assyria | Vastrim | | | 9632 |
| 86. | Affrica | Odraxti | | Order 29: RII | 4236 |
| 87. | Bactriani | Gomziam | | | 7635 |
| 88. | Asnan | Taoagla | | | 4632 |
| 89. | Phrygia | Gemnimb | | Order 30: TEX | 9636 |
| 90. | Creta | Advorpt | | | 7632 |
| 91. | Mauritania | Doxinal | | | 5632 |

| 0 | 6 | 7 | | 8 | 9 |
|---|---|---|---|---|---|
| 76. | | ARFAOLG | 12 | Ephraim | North N-W |
| 77. | 18489 | CADAAMP | 8 | Benjamin | North N-E |
| 78. | | ARFAOLG | 12 | Ephraim | North N-W |
| 79. | | ZIRACAH | 2 | Ruben | South |
| 80. | 22043 | ZARNAAH | 4 | Manasse | North |
| 81. | | GEBABAL | 5 | Asseir | East S-E |
| 82. | | LAVAVOTH | 10 | Gad | South S-E |
| 83. | 18066 | ZARZILG | 9 | Nephthalim | East N-E |
| 84. | | ZURCHOL | 6 | Simeon | South S-W |
| 85. | | HONONOL | 3 | Iehudah | West |
| 86. | 21503 | ZARNAAH | 4 | Manasse | North |
| 87. | | ARFAOLG | 12 | Ephraim | North N-W |
| 88. | | ARFAOLG | 12 | Ephraim | North N-W |
| 89. | | ZARNAAH | 4 | Manasse | North |
| 90. | 27532 | HONONOL | 3 | Iehudah | West |
| 91. | | ZURCHOL | 6 | Simeon | South S-W |

Hʜ

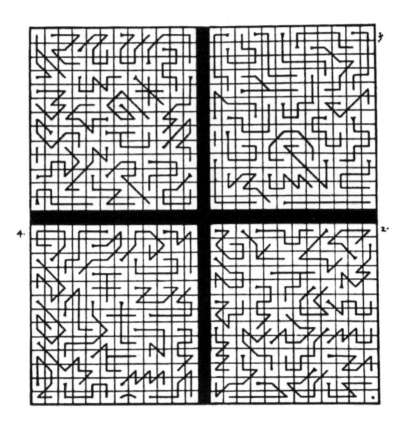

THE CHARACTERS UPON THE GREAT TABLE

# BOOK FIVE
# THE ANGELS OF THE FOUR QUARTERS

### CHAPTER I

### THE GREAT TABLE

This is the Great Table from which the Angels in this book have been derived.

# THE CORRECTED GREAT TABLE

☝

⚡ *This is the Great Table as reformed by Raphæl on the twentieth of April, 1587.*

♈

| r | Z | i | f | a | f | A | y | t | f | p | a | e | Z | a | O | A | d | u | p | t | D | n | i | m |
|---|---|---|---|---|---|---|---|---|---|---|---|---|---|---|---|---|---|---|---|---|---|---|---|---|
| a | r | d | Z | a | i | d | p | a | L | a | m | | a | a | b | c | o | o | r | o | m | e | b | b |
| c | z | o | n | s | a | r | o | Y | a | u | b | x | Z | o | p | c | o | n | x | m | a | f | G | m |
| Z | o | i | Z | t | z | o | P | a | c | o | C | a | n | h | o | d | D | i | a | f | e | a | o | c |
| S | i | p | a | s | o | m | r | b | x | n | h | r | p | a | t | A | x | i | o | U | s | P | s | Y |
| f | m | o | n | d | a | Z | d | i | a | r | i | p | S | a | a | i | x | a | a | r | U | r | o | i |
| o | r | o | i | b | A | h | a | o | z | p | i | | m | p | h | a | r | s | f | p | a | i | o | f |
| t | N | a | b | r | U | i | x | p | a | s | d | h | M | a | m | p | f | o | i | n | L | i | r | x |
| O | i | i | i | t | Z | p | a | f | O | a | i | | o | f | a | a | D | n | p | a | Z | a | p | a |
| A | b | a | m | o | o | o | a | C | u | c | a | C | p | a | L | c | o | i | d | x | P | a | c | n |
| N | a | o | c | O | Z | t | n | p | r | n | Z | o | n | d | a | x | N | z | i | U | a | a | s | a |
| o | c | a | n | m | a | p | o | t | r | o | i | m | i | i | d | P | o | n | s | d | A | s | p | i |
| S | h | i | a | f | r | a | p | m | z | o | x | a | x | r | i | n | h | t | a | r | n | d | i | ⌐ |
| m | o | b | i | t | | | a | Z | n | a | n | | n | a | n | Z | a | | | b | i | t | o | m |
| b | O | a | Z | a | R | o | p | h | a | R | a | a | d | o | n | p | a | Z | d | a | n | U | a | a |
| u | N | n | a | x | o | P | S | o | n | d | n | | o | f | o | a | G | e | o | o | b | a | u | a |
| a | i | p | r | a | n | o | o | m | a | p | p | m | O | P | a | m | n | o | U | G | m | d | n | m |
| o | r | p | m | n | i | n | p | b | e | a | f | o | a | p | f | s | Z | e | d | e | c | a | o | p |
| r | s | O | n | i | Z | i | r | f | e | m | u | C | S | c | m | i | o | o | n | A | m | f | o | x |
| i | z | i | n | r | C | Z | i | a | M | h | f | h | U | a | r | s | G | d | L | b | r | i | a | p |
| M | O | r | d | i | a | f | h | C | t | G | a | | o | i | P | t | e | a | a | p | D | o | c | e |
| O | c | a | n | c | h | i | a | s | o | m | c | p | p | s | u | a | c | N | r | Z | i | r | Z | a |
| A | r | b | i | z | m | i | i | p | i | z | | S | i | o | d | a | o | i | n | r | z | f | m |
| O | p | a | n | a | f | a | m | S | m | a | P | r | d | a | f | t | Z | d | n | a | d | i | r | e |
| d | O | f | o | P | i | n | i | a | n | b | a | a | d | i | x | o | m | o | n | s | i | o | s | p |
| r | x | P | a | o | c | s | i | z | i | x | p | x | O | o | D | p | z | i | A | p | a | n | f | i |
| a | x | t | i | r | U | a | s | t | r | i | m | e | r | p | o | a | n | n | q | A | C | r | a | r |

# THE GREAT CIRCLE OF THE QUARTERS

♉

**⅗** *The four triads are the Names of God extracted from the four lines of the holy spirit, which govern all creatures on the earth (both visible and invisible). They are carried upon twelve banners.*

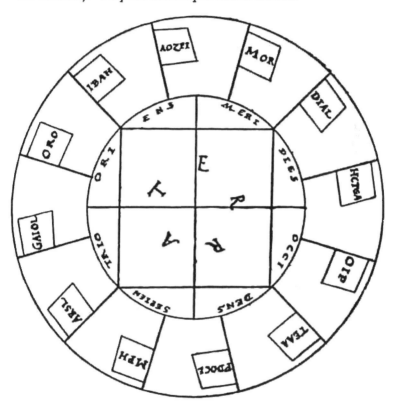

CHAPTER IV

## THE FUNDAMENTAL OBESANCE

❦

*This is the fundamental obesance to God, and the conjuration for obtaining the benign ministry of the good angels.*

IEOVAH ZEBAOTH, I, John Dee (your unworthy servant) most earnestly invoke and call upon your divine power, wisdom, and goodness. I humbly and faithfully seek your favour and assistance to me in all my deeds, words, and thoughts, and in the promoting, procuring, and mingling of your praise, honour, and glory. Through these , your twelve mystical Names: Oro, Ibah, Aozpi, Mor, Dial, Hctga, Oip, Teaa, Pdoce, Mph, Arsl, Gaiol, I conjure and pray most zealously to your divine and omnipotent majesty, that all your angelic spirits (whose mystical names are contained in this book, and whose offices are herein briefly noted) might be called from any and all parts of the universe, or at any time in my life, through the special domination and controlling power of your holy Names (which are also in this book). Let them come most quickly to me. Let them appear visibly, friendily, and peacefully to me. Let them remain visible according to my will. Let them vanish from me and from my sight when I so request. Let them give reverence and obedience before you and your 12 mystical Names. I command that they happily satisfy me in all things and at all times in my life, by accomplishing each and every one of my petitions—if not by one means, then by another—goodly, virtuously, and perfectly, with an excellent and thorough completeness, according to their virtues and powers, both general and unique, and by Your united ministry and office
O God . Amen.
Through you, Jesu Christe,
Amen
✠

120

## CHAPTER V
# THE TWENTY FOUR SENIORS
ȣ

*These are the twenty-four Seniors (mentioned in the* Apocalypse *of* Saint John) *whose names are compiled from the lines of the Father, the Son, and the Holy Ghost. The duty of these Good Angels is to impart knowledge and judgement in human affairs.*

| QUARTER | GOD NAME | SENIORS |
|---------|----------|---------|
| East | BATAIVA or BATAIVH | Abioro or Habioro |
| | | Aaoxaif |
| | | Htmorda |
| | | Haozpi or Ahaozpi |
| | | Hipotga |
| | | Autotar |
| South | ICZHHCA or ICZHHCL | Aidrom or Laidrom |
| | | Aczinor |
| | | Lzinopo |
| | | Lhctga or Alhctga |
| | | Lhiansa |
| | | Acmbicu |
| West | RAAGIOS or RAAGIOL | Srahpm or Lsrahpm |
| | | Saiinou |
| | | Laoaxrp |
| | | Lgaiol or Slgaiol |
| | | Ligdisa |
| | | Soaiznt |
| North | ELDPRNA or EDLPRNA | Ætpio or Aætpio |
| | | Adoeoet |
| | | Alndvod |
| | | Apdoce or Aapdoce |
| | | Arinnaq |
| | | Anodoin |

*This is the invitation to the six seniors of the East:*

 YOU SIX SENIORS OF THE EAST, POWERFUL AND FAITHFUL to the omnipotent God of our ministery, in the name of the same God (one and three), I say to you, ABIORO or HABIORO, AAOZAIF, HTMORDA, HAOZPI or AHAOZPI, HIPOTGA, AUTOTAR, through the divine Name by which you are particularly bound, the angelic Name BATAIVA or BATAIVH, I, John Dee, a faithful servant of the omnipotent God, amicably, earnestly, and confidently demand and beseech you to appear placidly, affably, and favourably before me, immediately and without delay, and henceforth at any time I wish, through all the remaining journey of my life, I beseech all of you, some of you, or whichever of you I name, united or divided, to grant all my petitions, and especially grant me Knowledge and Judgement in human affairs, and in all other things that are assigned to your Office and Ministry and that are accomplished by you, one and many. I command you to appear, to perform, and to complete, goodly, plainly, intelligibly, and perfectly, according to your Virtue, Power, and Office, and according to the capacity of your Ministry, entrusted and committed to you by the omnipotent God.

AMEN

Through the sacred Name of God

BATAIVA or BATAIVH

AMEN

✠

| | | | | | | | | | | | |
|---|---|---|---|---|---|---|---|---|---|---|---|
| r | Z | i | ( | a | ſ | A | u | t | ſ | ? | a |
| a | r | d | Z | a | i | d | ? | a | L | a | m |
| c | z | o | n | S | a | r | o | Y | o | u | b |
| C | o | i | Z | t | x | o | P | a | c | o | C |
| S | i | g | a | S | o | m | r | b | z | n | h |
| ſ | m | o | n | d | a | C | d | i | a | r | i |
| o | r | o | i | b | A | h | a | o | z | ? | i |
| c | N | a | b | r | V | i | x | g | a | z | d |
| O | i | i | t | Z | ? | a | ſ | O | a | i | |
| A | b | a | m | o | o | o | a | C | u | c | a |
| N | a | o | c | O | C | t | n | ? | r | a | Z |
| o | c | a | n | m | a | g | o | t | r | o | i |
| S | h | i | a | ſ | r | a | ? | m | z | o | x |

*This is the invitation to the six seniors of the South:*

YOU SIX SENIORS OF THE SOUTH, POWERFUL & FAITHFUL to the omnipotent God of our ministry, in the Name of the same God (one and three), I say to you, AIDROM or LAIDROM, ACZINOR, LZINOPO, LHCTGA or ALHCTGA, LHIANSA, ACMBICU, through the divine Name by which you are particularly bound, the angelic Name ICZHHCA or ICZHHCL, I, John Dee, a faithful servant of the omnipotent God, amicably ,earnestly, and confidently demand and beseech you to appear placidly, affably, and favourably before me , immediately and without delay, and henceforth at any time I wish, through all the remaining journey of my life, I beesech all of you, some of you, or whichever of you I name, united or divided, to grant all my petitions, and especially grant me Knowledge and Judgement in human affairs, and in all other things that are assigned to your Office and Ministry and that are accomplished by you, one and many. I command you to appear, to perform, and to complete, goodly, plainly, intelligibly, and perfectly, according to your Virtue, Power, and Office, and according to the capacity of your Ministry, entrusted and committed to you by the omnipotent God.

AMEN

Through the sacred Name of God

ICZHHCA or ICZHHCL

AMEN

✠

| b O | a | Z | a | R | o | p | h | a | R | a |
| u N | n | a | x | o | P | S | o | n | d | n |
| a i | g | r | a | n | o | o | m | a | g | g |
| o r | p | m | n | i | n | g | b | e | a | ſ |
| r s | O | n | i | Z | i | r | ſ | e | m | v |
| i z | i | n | r | C | z | i | a | M | h | ſ |
| M O | r | d | i | a | ſ | h | C | t | G | a |
| R O | c | a | n | c | h | i | a | s | o | m |
| A r | b | i | z | m | i | i | ſ | p | i | z |
| O p | a | n | a | B | a | m | S | m | a | L |
| d O | ſ | o | P | i | n | i | a | n | b | a |
| r x | p | a | o | c | S | i | z | i | x | p |
| a x | t | i | r | V | a | s | t | i | m |

*This is the invitation to the six Seniors of the West:*

 YOU SIX SENIORS OF THE WEST, POWERFUL & FAITHFUL to the omnipotent God of our ministry, in the Name of the same God (one and three), I say to you, SRAHPM or LSRAHPM, SAIINOU, LAOAXRP, LGAIOL or SLGAIOL, LIGDISA, SOAIZNT, through the divine Name by which you are particularly bound, the angelic Name RAAGIOS or RAAGIOL, I, John Dee, a faithful servant of the omnipotent God, amicably, earnestly, and confidently demand and beseech you to appear placidly, affably, and favourably before me, immediately and without delay, and henceforth at any time I wish, through all the remaining journey of my life, I beseech all of you, some of you, or whichever of you I name, united or divided, to grant all my petitions, and especially grant me Knowledge and Judgement in human affairs, and in all other things that are assigned to your Office and Ministry and that are accomplished by you, one and many. I command you to appear, to perform, and to complete, goodly, plainly, intelligibly, and perfectly, according to your Virtue, Power, and Office, and according to the capacity of your Ministry, entrusted and committed to you by the omnipotent God.

AMEN

Through the sacred Name of God

RAAGIOS or RAAGIOL

AMEN

✠

| | | | | | | | | | | |
|---|---|---|---|---|---|---|---|---|---|---|
| T | a | O | A | d | u | y | t | D | n | i | m |
| o | a | s | c | o | o | r | o | m | e | b | b |
| T | a | g | c | o | n | x | m | a | s | G | m |
| n | h | o | d | D | i | a | s | e | a | o | c |
| y | a | t | A | x | i | o | V | s | P | s | H |
| S | a | a | i | z | o | a | r | V | r | o | i |
| m | y | h | a | r | s | s | g | a | i | o | s |
| M | a | m | g | s | o | i | n | L | i | r | x |
| o | s | a | a | D | a | g | a | T | a | y | a |
| y | a | L | c | o | i | d | x | P | a | c | n |
| n | d | a | z | N | z | i | V | a | a | s | a |
| i | i | d | P | o | n | s | d | A | s | y | i |
| x | r | i | n | h | t | a | r | n | d | i | J |

*⚜This is the invitation to the six Seniors of the North:*

YOU SIX SENIORS OF THE NORTH, POWERFUL & FAITHFUL to the omnipotent God of our ministry, in the Name of the same God (one and three), I say to you, ÆTPIO or AÆTPIO, ADOBOET, ALNDVOD, APDOCE or AAPDOCE, ARINNAQ, ANODOIN, through the divine Name by which you are particularly bound, the angelic Name ELDPRNA or EDLPRNA, I, John Dee, a faithful servant of the omnipotent God, amicably, earnestly, and confidently demand and beseech you to appear placidly, affably, and favourably before me, immediately and without delay, and henceforth at any time I wish, through all the remaining journey of my life, I beseech all of you, some of you, or whichever of you I name, united or divided, to grant all my petitions, and especially grant me Knowledge and Judgement in human affairs, and in all other things that are assigned to your Office and Ministry and that are accomplished by you, one and many. I command you to appear, to perform, and to complete, goodly, plainly, intelligibly, and perfectly, according to your Virtue, Power, and Office, and according to the capacity of your Ministry, entrusted and committed to you by the omnipotent God.

AMEN
Through the sacred Name of God
ELDPRNA or EDLPRNA
AMEN
✠

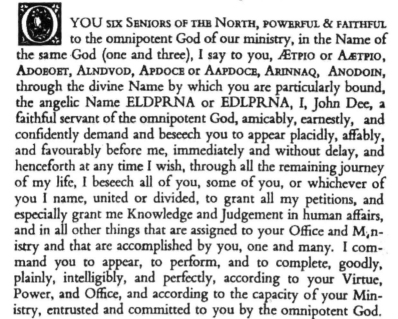

# THE ANGELS OF MEDICINE

❧

*These are the names of the sixteen good angels who are most skilled and powerful in medicine and in the curing of diseases. Also shown are the sixteen cacodemons who can inflict diseases, &c.*

| Quarter | God Name | Angels | Caco-Demons | God Names Reversed |
|---|---|---|---|---|
| East | IDOIGO | Czns or Czons | Xcz | OGIODI |
|  | ARDZA | Tott or Toitt | Ato | AZDRA |
|  |  | Sias or Sigas | Rsi |  |
|  |  | Fmnd or Fmond | Pfm |  |
| South | ANGPOI | Aira or Aigra | Xai | IOPGNA |
|  | VNNAX | Ormn or Orpmn | Aor | XANNV |
|  |  | Rsni or Rsoni | Rrs |  |
|  |  | Iznr or Izinr | Pi |  |
| West | OLGOTA | Taco or Tagco | Mta | ATOGLO |
|  | OALCO | Nhdd or Nhodd | Onh | OCLAO |
|  |  | Paax or Patax | Cfa |  |
|  |  | Saiz or Saaiz | Hsa |  |
| North | NOALMR | Opmn or Opamn | Mop | RMLAON |
|  | OLOAG | Apst or Aplst | Oap | GAOLO |
|  |  | Scio or Scmio | Csc |  |
|  |  | Vasg or Varsg | Hua |  |

*This is the invitation to the four good angels of the East, who are most skilled and powerful in medicine and the cure of diseases:*

YOU ANGELS OF LIGHT CZNS OR CZONS, TOTT OR TOITT, SIAS or SIGAS, FMND or FMOND, dwelling in the Eastern part of the universe, powerful in the administering of the strong and healthy medicine of God and in the dispensing of cures: In the Name of the omnipotent, living, and true God, I, John Dee, by the grace of God of the Celestial City of Jerusalem, and through the reverence and obedience which you owe to the same, our God, and through these, His divine and mystical Names, IDOIGO and ARDZA, I vehemently and faithfully require of you, one and all to come before me, I beseech you, at whatever moment of time I wish for the duration of my natural life. I summon you by the Names of God, IDOIGO and ARDZA, to perform, to accomplish, and to complete all my requests, abundantly, excellently, thoroughly, pleasantly, plentily, and perfectly, in any and all things, through every possible medicine and through the peculiar strength and power of your office and ministry.

Through the Sacrosanct Names of God
IDOIGO and ARDZA
AMEN
✠

| r | Z | i | ( | a |
|---|---|---|---|---|
| a | r | 6 | Z | a |
| c | z | o | n | s |
| ꞇ | o | i | ꞇ | t |
| S | i | 9 | a | s |
| ꝩ | m | o | n | 6 |

*❧This is the invitation to the four good angels of the South, who are most skilled and powerful in medicine and the cure of diseases:*

YOU ANGELS OF LIGHT, AIRA OR AIGRA, ORMN OR ORPMN, RSNI OR RSONI, IZNR OR IZINR, dwelling in the Southern part of the universe, powerful in the administering of the strong and healthy medicine of God and in the dispensing of cures: In the Name of the omnipotent, living, and true God, I, John Dee, by the grace of the God of the Celestial City of Jerusalem, and through the reverence and obedience which you owe to the same, our God, and through these, His divine and mystical Names, ANGPOI and VNNAX, I vehemently and faithfully require of you, one and all to come before me, I beseech you, at whatever moment of time I wish for the duration of my natural life. I summon you by the Names of God, ANGPOI & VNNAX, to perform, to accomplish, and to complete all my requests, abundantly, excellently, thoroughly, pleasantly, and perfectly, in any and all things, through every possible medicine, and through the peculiar strength and power of your office and ministry.

Through the Sacrosanct Names of God

ANGPOI and VNNAX

AMEN

✠

| b | O | a | Z | a |
|---|---|---|---|---|
| u | N | n | a | x |
| a | i | g | r | a |
| o | r | p | m | n |
| r | s | O | n | i |
| i | x | i | n | r |

I

*This is the invitation to the four good angels of the West, who are most skilled and powerful in medicine and the cure of diseases:*

YOU ANGELS OF LIGHT, TACO OR TAGCO, NHDD OR NHODD, PAAX or PATAX, SAIZ or SAAIZ, dwelling in the Western part of the universe, powerful in the administering of the strong and healthy medicine of God and in the dispensing of cures: In the Name of the omnipotent, living, and true God, I, John Dee, by the grace of the God of the Celestial City of Jerusalem, and through the reverence and obedience which you owe to the same, our God, and through these, His divine and mystical Names, OLGOTA and OALCO, I vehemently and faithfully require of you, one and all to come before me, I beseech you, at whatever moment of time I wish for the duration of my natural life. I summon you by the Names of God, OLGOTA and OALCO, to perform, to accomplish, and to complete all my requests, abundantly, excellently, thoroughly, pleasantly, plentily, and perfectly, in any and all things, through every possible medicine, and through the peculiar strength and power of your office and ministry.

Through the Sacrosanct Names of God
OLGOTA and OALCO
AMEN
✠

*This is the invitation to the four good angels of the North, who are most skilled and powerful in medicine and the cure of diseases:*

YOU ANGELS OF LIGHT, OPMN OR OPAMN, APST OR APLST, SCIO OR SCMIO, VASQ OR VARSQ, dwelling in the Northern part of the universe, powerful in the administering of the strong and healthy medicine of God and in the dispensing of cures: In the Name of the omnipotent , living, and true God, I, John Dee, by the grace of the God of the Celestial City of Jerusalem, and through the reverence and obedience which you owe to the same, our God, and through these, His divine and mystical Names, NOALMR and OLOAG, I vehemently and faithfully require of you, one and all to come before me, I beseech you, at whatever moment of time I wish for the duration of my natural life. I summon you by the Names of God, NOALMR and OLOAG, to perform, to accomplish, and to complete all my requests, abundantly, excellently, thoroughly, pleasantly, plentily, and perfectly, in all things, through every possible medicine, and through the peculiar strength and power of your office and ministry.

Through the Sacrosanct Names of God
NOALMR and OLOAG
AMEN
✠

| d | o | n | p | a |
|---|---|---|---|---|
| o | l | o | a | G |
| O | P | a | m | n |
| a | g | l | s | T |
| s | c | m | i | o |
| V | a | r | s | G |

IJ

# THE ANGELS OF PRECIOUS STONES

❧

*These are the names of the sixteen good angels who are powerful &
learned in the finding, collection, use, and virtues of metals, and in the
coagulations and powers of jewels.*

| Quarter | God Names | Angels | Caco-Demons | God Names Reversed |
|---|---|---|---|---|
| East | LLACZA | Oyub or Oyaub | Xoy | AZCALL |
| | PALAM | Paoc or Pacoc | Apa | MALAP |
| | | Rbnh or Rbznh | Rrb | |
| | | Diri or Diari | Pdi | |
| South | ANÆEM | Omgg or Omagg | Xom | MEEANA |
| | SONDN | Gbal or Gbeal | Agb | NDNOS |
| | | Rlmu or Rlemu | Rrl | |
| | | Iahl or Iamhl | Pia | |
| West | NELAPR | Magm or Malg | Mma | RPALEN |
| | OMEBB | Leoc or Leaoc | Ole | BBEMO |
| | | Vssn or Vspsn | Cvs | |
| | | Rvoi or Rvroi | Hrv | |
| North | VADALI | Gmnm or Gmdnm | Mgm | ILADAV |
| | OBARA | Ecop or Ecaop | Oec | AVABO |
| | | Amox or Amlox | Cam | |
| | | Brap or Briap | Hbr | |

*This is the invitation of the four good angels of the East, who are powerful and learned in metals and jewels:*

YOU FOUR ANGELS OF LIGHT, FAITHFUL IN THE MINISTRY of God (our Creator), OYUB or OYAUB, PAOC or PACOC, RBNH or RBZNH, DIRI or DIARI, lords in the Eastern part of the universe, and who (out of the peculiar gifts and dispensations of God) are powerful and learned in the lore of ore-veins, the finding of metal and treasure hoards, the uses and virtues of metals, the coagulation and magical properties of jewels, the places where metals and jewels are gathered, as well as their natures, properties, virtues, and uses, both secret and arcane: I, John Dee, the humble and devoted servant of the omnipotent, living, and true God, IEOVA ZEBOATH, through the inevitable power which is known to the same, our God, in these Names, LLACZA and PALAM, to whom you owe reverence and obedience, I vehemently and confidently require of you , one and all, that, through the whole of my remaining life at whatever time I wish, you come and appear before me, benignly, placidly, visibly, and pleasantly, and be favourable unto me. I beseech thee, one and all, to complete and to make perfect all my petitions for intended deeds, most swiftly, manifestly, certainly, immaculately, and plentifully. Yet I bind myself by this condition, that all my demands, totally or for the most part, be mindful of your peculiar skills, strengths, faculties, and powers over metals and jewels. By the speaking of the divine Names, LLACZA and PALAM, I call and command you, one and all.

AMEN

Through the speaking of the holy & mystical Names of God
LLACZA and PALAM

AMEN

✠

| u | t | s | ſ | a |
|---|---|---|---|---|
| y | a | L | a | m |
| o | Y | o | u | b |
| P | a | c | o | C |
| r | b | z | n | h |
| d | i | a | r | i |

*꙾This is the invitation of the four good angels of the South, who are powerful and learned in metals and jewels:*

 YOU FOUR ANGELS OF LIGHT, FAITHFUL IN THE MINISTRY of God (our Creator), OMGG or OMAGG, GBAL or GBEAL, RLMU or RLEMU, IAHL or IAMHL, lords in the Southern part of the universe, and who (out of the peculiar gifts and dispensations of God) are powerful and learned in the lore of ore-veins, the finding of metals and treasure hoards, the uses and virtues of metals, the coagulation and magical properties of jewels, the places where metals and jewels are gathered, as well as their natures, properties, virtues, and uses, both secret and arcane: I, John Dee, the humble and devoted servant of the omnipotent, living, and true God, IEOVA ZEBOATH, through the inevitable power which is known to the same, our God, in these Names, ANÆEM and SONDN, to whom you owe reverence and obedience, I vehemently and confidently require of you, one and all, that, through the whole of my remaining life at whatever time I wish, you come and appear before me, benignly, placidly, visibly, and pleasantly, and be favourable unto me. I beseech thee, one and all, to complete and to make perfect all my petitions for intended deeds, most swiftly, manifestly, certainly, immaculately, and plentifully. Yet I bind myself by this condition, that all my demands, totally or for the most part, be mindful of your peculiar skills, strengths, faculties, and powers over metals and jewels. By the speaking of the divine Names, ANÆEN and SONDN, I call and command you, one and all.

AMEN

Through the speaking of the holy and mystical Names of God
ANÆEM and SONDN

AMEN

☨

| p | h | a | R | a |
|---|---|---|---|---|
| S | o | n | d | n |
| o | m | a | g | g |
| g | b | e | a | ſ |
| r | ſ | e | m | v |
| i | a | M | h | ſ |

*⚜This is the invitation of the four good angels of the West, who are powerful and learned in metals and jewels:*

 YOU FOUR ANGELS OF LIGHT, FAITHFUL IN THE MINISTRY of God (our Creator), MAGM or MALGM, LEOC or LEAOC, VSSN or VSPSN, RVOI or RVROI, lords in the Western part of the universe, and who (out of the peculiar gifts and dispensations of God) are powerful and learned in the lore of ore-veins, the finding of metals and treasure hoards, the uses and virtues of metals, the coagulation and magical properties of jewels, the places where metals and jewels are gathered, as well as their natures, properties, virtues, and uses, both secret and arcane: I, John Dee, the humble and devoted servant of the omnipotent, living, and true God, IEOVA ZEBOATH, through the inevitable power which is known to the same, our God, in these Names, NELAPR and OMEBB, to whom you owe reverence and obedience, I vehemently and confidently require of you , one and all, that, through the whole of my remaining life at whatever time I wish, you come and appear before me, benignly, placidly, visibly, and pleasantly, and be favourable unto me. I beseech thee, one and all, to complete and make perfect all my petitions for intended deeds, most swiftly, manifestly, certainly, immacultely, and plentifully. Yet I bind myself by this condition, that all my demands, totally or for the most part, be mindful of your peculiar skills, strengths, faculties, and powers over metals and jewels. By the speaking of the divine Names, NALAPR and OMEBB, I call and command you, one and all.

AMEN

Through the speaking of the holy and mystical Names of God
NELAPR and OMEBB

AMEN

✠

*This is the invitation of the four good angels of the North, who are powerful and learned in metals and jewels:*

 YOU FOUR ANGELS OF LIGHT, FAITHFUL IN THE MINISTRY of God (our Creator), GMNM or GMDNM, ECOP or ECAOP, AMOX or AMLOX, BRAP or BRIAP, lords in the Northern part of the universe, and who (out of the peculiar gifts and dispensations of God) are powerful and learned in the lore of ore-veins, the finding of metals and treasure hoards, the uses and virtues of metals, the coagulation and magical properties of jewels, the places where metals and jewels are gathered, as well as their natures, properties, virtues, and uses, both secret and arcane: I, John Dee, the humble and devoted servant of the omnipotent, living, and true God, IEOVA ZEBOATH, through the inevitable ower which is known to the same, our God, in these Names, VADALI and OBAVA, to whom you owe reverence and obedience, I vehemently and confidently require of you, one and all, that, through the whole of my remaining life at whatever time I wish, you come and appear before me, benignly, placidly, visibly, and pleasantly, and be favourable unto me. I beseech thee, one and all, to complete and make perfect all my petitions for intended deeds, most swiftly, manifestly, certainly, immaculately, and plentifully. Yet I bind myself by this condition, that all my demands, totally or for the most part, be mindful of your peculiar skills, strengths, faculties, and powers over metals and jewels. By the speaking of the divine Names, VADALI and OBAVA, I call and command you, one and all.

AMEN

Through the speaking of the holy and mystical Names of God
VADALI and OBAVA

AMEN

✠

| a | n | V | a | a |
|---|---|---|---|---|
| o | b | a | u | a |
| G | m | d | n | m |
| e | c | a | o | p |
| A | m | s | o | x |
| b | r | i | a | p |

# THE ANGELS OF TRANSFORMATION

ȣ

*These are the names of the sixteen good angels who are powerful
and learned in Transformation; also shown are the names of the sixteen cacodemons.*

| Quarter | God Names | Angels | Caco-Demons | God Names Reversed |
|---------|-----------|--------|-------------|--------------------|
| East | AIAOAI OIIIT | Abmo or Abamo<br>Naco or Naoco<br>Ocnm or Ocanm<br>Shal or Shail | Cab<br>Ona<br>Moc<br>Ash | IAOAIA<br>TIIIO |
| South | CBALPT ARBIZ | Opna or Opana<br>Doop or Dolop<br>Rxao or Rxpao<br>Axir or Axtir | Cop<br>Odo<br>Mrx<br>Aax | TPLABC<br>ZIBRA |
| West | MALADI OLAAD | Paco or Palco<br>Ndzn or Ndazn<br>Iipo or Iidpo<br>Xrnh or Xrinh | Rpa<br>And<br>Xii<br>Exr | IDALAM<br>DAALO |
| North | VOLXDO SIODA | Datt or Dabtt<br>Diom or Dixom<br>Oopz or Oodpz<br>Rgan or Rgoan | Rda<br>Adi<br>Xoo<br>Erg | ODXLOV<br>ADIOS |

*§ This is the invitation of the four good angels of the East, who are learned and powerful in Transformation:*

YOU FOUR GOOD AND TRUE ANGELS OF GOD (OUR CRE-ator), ABMO or ABAMO, NACO or NAOCO, OCNM or OCANM, SHAL or SHIAL, who rule in the Eastern part of the world, who received of God in your creation the singular strength, true knowledge, and perfect absolute power of Trans-formation as your duty and office, that you might impart and make manifest unto men (as preordained by the same, our God) this true knowledge and perfect power, to the praise, honour, and glory of God. Therefore, I, John Dee, the devoted servant of the same, our God and Creator, truly, diligently, and faithfully desiring to praise, honour, and glorify in God, do vehemently demand and confidently beseech you, one and all, to bring to pass and amplify amongst men this your aforementioned true knowledge, through these mystical Names of God (pre-eminen-tly and predominantly peculiar to you): AIAOAI and OIIIT. I, John Dee, demand that you appear benignly, placidly, and vis-ibly to me, at whatever moment in time I should choose, for all the remaining time of my life, and moreover I demand that you deign to be friendly and favourable unto me. I, John Dee, de-mand that you (one and all), immediately and without delay, perfectly accomplish, manifestly discharge, plainly complete, and plentily make perfect each and every one of my petitions, by whatever means necessary, that concern or respect your skill, knowledge and power of Transformations, no matter when I shall require it of you, through these Names of our God, here rehearsed: AIAOAI and OIIIT.

AMEN

Through these sacred and mystical Names of God

AIAOAI and OIIIT

AMEN

☩

| c | N | a | b | r |
|---|---|---|---|---|
| O | i | i | i | t |
| A | b | a | m | o |
| N | a | o | c | O |
| o | c | a | n | m |
| S | h | i | a | ſ |

*⚜ This is the invitation of the four good angels of the South, who are learned and powerful in Transformation:*

 YOU FOUR GOOD AND TRUE ANGELS OF GOD (OUR CRE-ator), OPNA or OPANA, DOOP or DOLOP, RXAO or RXPAO, AXIR or AXTIR, who rule in the Southern part of the world, who received of God in your creation the singular strength, true knowledge, and perfect absolute power of Transformation as your duty and office, that you might impart and make manifest unto men (as preordained by the same, our God) this true knowledge and perfect power, to the praise, honour, and glory of God. Therefore, I, John Dee, the devoted servant of the same, our God and Creator, truly, diligently, and faithfully desiring to praise, honour, and glorify in God, do vehemently demand and confidently beseech you, one and all, to bring to pass and amplify amongst men this your aforementioned true knowledge, through these mystical Names of God (pre-eminently and predominately peculiar to you): CBALPT and ARBIZ. I, John Dee, demand that you appear benignly, placidly, and visibly to me, at whatever moment in time I should choose, for all the remaining time of my life, and moreover I demand that you deign to be friendly and favourable unto me. I, John Dee, demand that you (one and all), immediately and without delay, perfectly accomplish, manifestly discharge, plainly complete, and plentily make perfect each and every one of my petitions, by whatever means necessary, that concern or respect your skill, knowledge and power of Transformations, no matter when I shall require it of you, through these Names of our God, here rehearsed: CBALPT and ARBIZ.

AMEN

Through these sacred and mystical Names of God

CBALPT and ARBIZ

AMEN

✠

| R | O | c | a | n |
|---|---|---|---|---|
| A | r | b | i | z |
| O | p | a | n | a |
| d | O | ſ | o | P |
| r | x | p | a | o |
| a | x | t | i | r |

*⚜This is the invitation of the four good angels of the West, who are learned and powerful in Transformation:*

YOU FOUR GOOD AND TRUE ANGELS OF GOD (OUR CREator), PACO or PALCO, NDZN or NDAZN, IIPO or IIDPO, XRNH or XRINH, who rule in the Western part of the world, who received of God in your creation the singular strength, true knowledge, and perfect absolute power of Transformation as your duty and office, that you might impart and make manifest unto men (as preordained by the same, our God) this true knowledge and perfect power, to the praise, honour, and glory of God. Therefore, I, John Dee, the devoted servant of the same, our God and Creator, truly, diligently, and faithfully desiring to praise, honour, and glorify in God, do vehemently demand and confidently beseech you, one and all, to bring to pass and amplify amongst men this your aforementioned true knowledge, through these mystical Names of God (pre-eminently and predominatly peculiar to you): MALADI and OLAAD. I, John Dee, demand that you appear benignly, placidly, and visibly to me, at whatever moment in time I should choose, for all the remaining time of my life, and moreover I demand that you deign to be friendly and favourable unto me. I, John Dee, demand that you (one and all), immediately and without delay, perfectly accomplish, manifestly discharge, plainly complete, and plentily make perfect each and every one of my petitions, by whatever means necessary, that concern or respect your skill, knowledge and power of Transformations, no matter when I shall require it of you, through these Names of our God, here rehearsed: MALADI and OLAAD.

AMEN

Through these sacred and mystical Names of God

MALADI and OLAAD

AMEN

✠

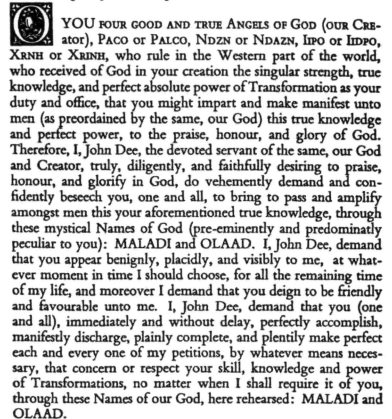

*This is the invitation of the four good angels of the North, who are learned and powerful in Transformation:*

YOU OUR GOOD AND TRUE ANGELS OF GOD (OUR CREator), DATT or DABTT, DIOM or DIXOM, OOPZ or OODPZ, RGAN or RGOAN, who rule in the Northern part of the world, who received of God in your creation the singular strength, true knowledge, and perfect absolute power of Transformation as your duty and office, that you might impart and make manifest unto men (as preordained by the same, our God) this true knowledge and perfect power, to the praise, honour, and glory of God. Therefore, I, John Dee, the devoted servant of the same, our God and Creator, truly, diligently, and faithfully desiring to praise, honour, and glorify in God, do vehemently demand and confidently beseech you, one and all, to bring to pass and amplify amongst men this your aforementioned true knowledge, through these mystical Names of God (pre-eminently and predominantly peculiar to you): VOLXDO and SIODA. I, John Dee, demand that you appear benignly, placidly, and visibly to me, at whatever moment in time I should choose, for all the remaining time of my life, and moreover I demand that you deign to be friendly and favourable unto me. I, John Dee, demand that you (one and all), immediately and without delay, perfectly accomplish, manifestly discharge, plainly complete, and plentily make perfect each and every one of my petitions, by whatever means necessary, that concern or respect your skill, knowledge and power of Transformations, no matter when I shall require it of you, through these Names of our God, here rehearsed: VOLXDO & SIODA.

AMEN

Through these sacred and mystical Names of God
VOLXDO and SIODA

AMEN

✠

| p | s | u | a | c |
|---|---|---|---|---|
| S | i | o | d | a |
| d | a | ſ | t | Z |
| d | i | x | o | m |
| O | o | D | p | x |
| r | g | o | a | n |

## CHAPTER IX

# THE ANGELS OF THE FOUR ELEMENTS

ꝏ

*These are the names of the sixteen good angels who liveth in and knoweth the quality and use of all four elements; also shown are the names of the sixteen cacodemons.*

| QTR. | GOD NAME | ANGELS | ELMNT | CACO-DEMONS | GOD NAMES REVERSED |
|------|----------|--------|-------|-------------|--------------------|
| E. | AOVRRZ | Acca or Acvca | Air | Cac | ZRRVOA |
|    | ALOAI | Npat or Nprat | Watr | Onp | IAOLA |
|    |       | Otoi or Otroi | Erth | Mot | |
|    |       | Pmox or Pmzox | Fire | Apm | |
| S. | SPMNIR | Msal or Msmal | Air | Cms | RINMPS |
|    | ILPIZ | Iaba or Ianba | Watr | Oia | ZIPLI |
|    |       | Izxp or Izixp | Erth | Miz | |
|    |       | Stim or Strim | Fire | Ast | |
| W. | IAAASD | Xpen or Xpæn | Air | Rxp | DSAAAI |
|    | ATAPA | Vasa or Vaasa | Watr | Ara | APATA |
|    |       | Dapi or Daspi | Erth | Xda | |
|    |       | Rnil or Rndil | Fire | Ern | |
| N. | RZIONR | Adre or Adire | Air | Rad | RNIOZR |
|    | NRZFM | Sisp or Siosp | Watr | Asi | MFZRN |
|    |       | Pali or Panli | Erth | Xpa | |
|    |       | Acar or Acrar | Fire | Eac | |

K

*This is the invitation to the four good angels of the East, each of whom knows all the creatures living in one element and their use:*

YOU Angels of God, flowing with truth & goodness, I call you , Acca or Acvca, Npat or Nprat, Otoi or Otroi, Pmox or Pmzox, who rule in the Eastern part of the world: so that each one of you, out of the four great elements or sources of the world might wield the duty or office peculiar to him, and his unique skill, knowledge, power, and authority: O you, Acca or Acvca, bright angel that liveth in the Air of the East, you who hath vision of all its diverse qualities and who perfectly perceives what uses God created in them for Man; And you, O illustrious Npat or Nprat, who liveth in the Water of the East, who truly knoweth its quality and use; And you, O distinguished Otoi or Otroi, who liveth in the Earth of the East, you who knoweth exactly its varied qualities and to what uses it was created by our God; And finally you, Pmox or pmzox, shining angel of God, who liveth in the most secret Fire of the East, and who hath plentiful knowledge of its efficacy and vital properties; O All of you, faithful to God and ministers of our Creator, you who dwelleth in the Eastern part of the world, you who knoweth the arcane secrets of the four elements, conceded, assigned, and deputed to you by our omnipotent Creator, and who, to the praise, honour, and glory of God and out of your great charity towards the human race art able to impart and make manifest these great things and (by the approval of God) bring forth those things that are asked of you. Therefore, I, John Dee, a Lover and Seeker for these secrets (to the praise, honour and glory of our God), in the Name of the same, our God and Creator, I humbly supplicate you, one and all. And through these holy Names of God, AOVRRZ and ALOAI, I require and confidently petition that, at whatever time of my future life (from this very hour) that I should call or summon one, any, or all of you, you appear conspicuous and visible to me in a goodly form. And through these holy Names of God, AOVRRZ and ALOAI, I require that you benignly consent, clearly discharge, lovingly fulfil, and perfectly make perfect, each and every one of my petitions (respecting and concerning your aforementioned unique offices, knowledges, and powers), satisfyingly, satisfactorily, plentily, and perfectly. AMEN

AMEN

Through these reverend and mystical Names of God

AOVRRZ and ALOAI

AMEN

| x | g | a | z | d |
|---|---|---|---|---|
| a | Y | O | a | i |
| a | C | u | c | a |
| n | g | r | a | C |
| o | t | r | o | i |
| g | m | z | o | x |

*This is the invitation to the four good angels of the South, each of whom knows all the creatures living in one element and their use:*

YOU Angels of God, flowing with truth & good-ness, I call you, Msal or Msmal, Iaba or Ianba, Ixzp or Izixp, Stim or Strim, who rule in the Southern part of the world: so that each one of you, out of the four great elements or sources of the world might wield the duty or office peculiar to him, and his unique skill, knowledge, power, and authority: O you, Msal or Msmal, bright angel that liveth in the Air of the South, you who hath vision of all its diverse qualities and who perfectly perceives what uses God created in them for Man; And you, O illustrious Iaba or Ianba, who liveth in the Water of the South, who truly knoweth its quality and use; And you, O distinguished Izxp or Izixp, who liveth in the Earth of the South, you who knoweth exactly its varied qualities and to what uses it was created by our God; And finally you , Stim or Strim, shining angel of God, who liveth in the most secret Fire of the South, and who hath plentiful knowledge of its efficacy and vital properties: O All of you, faithful to God and ministers of our Creator, you who dwelleth in the Southern part of the world, you who knoweth the arcane secrets of the four elements, con-ceded, assigned, and deputed to you by our omnipotent Creator, and who, to the praise, honour, and glory of God and out of your great charity towards the human race art able to impart and make manifest these great things and (by the approval of God) bring forth those things that are asked of you. Therefore, I, John Dee, a Lover and Seeker for these secrets (to the praise, honour and glory of our God), in the Name of the same, our God and Creator, I humbly supplicate you, one and all. And through these holy Names of God, SPMNIR and ILPIZ, I re-quire and confidently petition that, at whatever time of my fu-ture life (from this very hour) that I should call or summon one, any, or all of you, you appear conspicuous and visible to me in a goodly form. And through these holy Names of God, SPMNIR and ILPIZ, I require that you benignly consent, clearly discharge, lovingly fulfil, and perfectly make perfect, each and every one of my petitions (respecting and concerning your aforementioned unique offices, knowledges and powers), satisfyingly, satisfactorily, plentily and perfectly. AMEN

AMEN

Through these reverend and mystical Names of God

SPMNIR and ILPIZ

AMEN

✠

| | | | | |
|---|---|---|---|---|
| i | a | s | o | m |
| i | f | p | i | z |
| m | S | m | a | l |
| i | a | n | b | a |
| i | z | i | x | p |
| s | t | r | i | m |

*This is the invitation to the four good angels of the West, each of whom knows all the creatures living in one element and their use:*

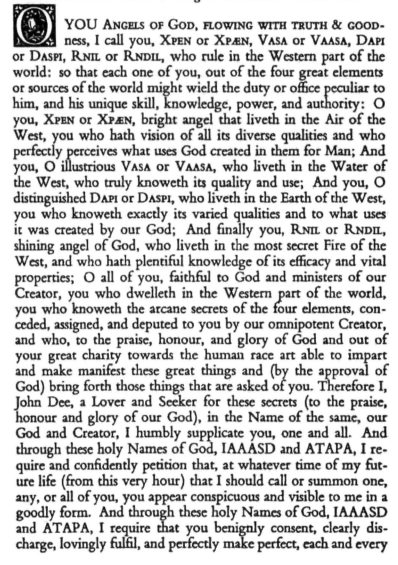 YOU ANGELS OF GOD, FLOWING WITH TRUTH & GOODness, I call you, XPEN or XPÆN, VASA or VAASA, DAPI or DASPI, RNIL or RNDIL, who rule in the Western part of the world: so that each one of you, out of the four great elements or sources of the world might wield the duty or office peculiar to him, and his unique skill, knowledge, power, and authority: O you, XPEN or XPÆN, bright angel that liveth in the Air of the West, you who hath vision of all its diverse qualities and who perfectly perceives what uses God created in them for Man; And you, O illustrious VASA or VAASA, who liveth in the Water of the West, who truly knoweth its quality and use; And you, O distinguished DAPI or DASPI, who liveth in the Earth of the West, you who knoweth exactly its varied qualities and to what uses it was created by our God; And finally you, RNIL or RNDIL, shining angel of God, who liveth in the most secret Fire of the West, and who hath plentiful knowledge of its efficacy and vital properties; O all of you, faithful to God and ministers of our Creator, you who dwelleth in the Western part of the world, you who knoweth the arcane secrets of the four elements, conceded, assigned, and deputed to you by our omnipotent Creator, and who, to the praise, honour, and glory of God and out of your great charity towards the human race art able to impart and make manifest these great things and (by the approval of God) bring forth those things that are asked of you. Therefore I, John Dee, a Lover and Seeker for these secrets (to the praise, honour and glory of our God), in the Name of the same, our God and Creator, I humbly supplicate you, one and all. And through these holy Names of God, IAAASD and ATAPA, I require and confidently petition that, at whatever time of my future life (from this very hour) that I should call or summon one, any, or all of you, you appear conspicuous and visible to me in a goodly form. And through these holy Names of God, IAAASD and ATAPA, I require that you benignly consent, clearly discharge, lovingly fulfil, and perfectly make perfect, each and every

one of my petitions (respecting and concerning your aforementioned unique offices, knowledges and powers), satisfyingly, satisfactorily, plentily, and perfectly. AMEN
          AMEN
Through these reverend and mystical Names of God
          IAAASD and ATAPA
          AMEN
          ✠

*This is the invitation to the four good angels of the North, each of whom knows all the creatures living in one element and their use:*

YOU Angels of God, flowing with truth & good-ness, I call you , Adre or Adire, Sisp or Siosp, Pali or Panli, Acar or Acrar, who rule in the Northern part of the world: so that each one of you, out of the four great elements or sources of the world might wield the duty or office peculiar to him, and his unique skill, knowledge, power, and authority: O you, Adre or Adire, bright angel that liveth in the Air of the North, you who hath vision of all its diverse qualities and who perfectly perceives what uses God created in them for Man, And you, O illustrious Sisp or Siosp, who liveth in the Water of the North, who truly knoweth its quality and use; And you, O distinguished Pali or Panli, who liveth in the Earth of the North, you who knoweth exactly its varied qualities and to what uses it was created by our God; And finally you, Acar or Acrar, shining angel of God, who liveth in the most secret Fire of the North, and who hath plentiful knowledge of its efficacy and vital properties; O All of you, faithful to God and ministers of our Creator, you who dwelleth in the Northern part of the world, you who knoweth the arcane secrets of the four elements, conceded, assigned, and deputed to you by our omnipotent Creator, and who, to the praise, honour, and glory of God and out of your great charity towards the human race art able to impart and make manifest these grest things and (by the approval of God) bring forth those things that are asked of you. Therefore I, John Dee, a Lover and Seeker for these secrets (to the praise, honour and glory of our God), in the Name of the same, our Creator and God, I humbly supplicate you, one and all. And through these holy Names of God, RZIONR and NRZFM, I require and confidently petition that, at whatever time of my future life (from this very hour) that I should call or summon one, any, or all of you, you appear conspicuous and visible to me in a goodly form. And through these holy Names of God, RZIONR and NRZFM, I require that you benignly consent, clearly discharge, lovingly fulfil, and perfectly make perfect, each and every one of my petitions (respecting and concerning your aforementioned unique offices , knowledges, and powers), satisfyingly, satisfactorily, plentily, and perfectly. AMEN

AMEN

Through these reverend and mystical Names of God
RZIONR and NRZFM

AMEN

✠

| Z | i | r | Z | a |
|---|---|---|---|---|
| n | r | z | ſ | m |
| a | d | i | r | e |
| s | i | o | s | ρ |
| ρ | a | n | ſ | i |
| A | C | r | a | r |

## CHAPTER X

## THE ANGELS OF NATURAL SUBSTANCES

♉

*These are the names of the sixteen good angels who are most power-ful and skilled in the mixing together of natural substances.\**

| QUARTER | GOD NAME | ANGELS | LETTER FROM THE CROSS |
|---------|----------|--------|------------------------|
| East | ERZLA | RZLA<br>ZLAR<br>LARZ<br>ARZL | I |
| South | EBOZA | BOZA<br>OZAB<br>ZABO<br>ABOZ | A |
| West | ATAAD | TAAD<br>AADT<br>ADTA<br>DTAA | O |
| North | ADOPA | DOPA<br>OPAD<br>PADO<br>ADOP | N |

\* Commixtionibus Naturarum

*⚜This is the invitation to the four good Angels of the East, who are powerful and learned in the mixing together of natural substances:*

 YOU four, faithful & truthful ministers of omnipotent God, (your Creator) Rzla, Zlar, Larz, Arzl, who are in the Eastern part of the world, and are powerful and skilled in the mixing together of natural substances: I, John Dee, devoted servant of the same, our Creator, and through the omnipotence of the same, our Creator, and through this mystical Name of our God, ERZLA, humbly require, and vehemently petition, from you, one and all, that at whatever time of my future life that I invoke or call your name, through this mystic Name of God, ERZLA, that you will come to me and appear visibly and personally, and deign to be friendly and favourable unto me. I require that you discharge, implement, and make perfect, benignly, plentily, plainly, and perfectly any and all of my petitions concerning the mixing together of natural substances and other natural secrets, which our Creator hath committed to your understanding, intelligence, and disposition and, as it were, appointed you as His officers and ministers. Amen

Through this Holy and Mystical Name of God

ERZLA

Amen

✠

| r | Z | i | ( | a |
|---|---|---|---|---|
| a | r | δ | Z | a |
| c | z | o | n | s |
| ζ | o | i | ζ | t |
| S | i | 9 | a | s |
| ſ | ɱ | o | n | δ |

*This is the invitation to the four good angels of the South, who are powerful and learned in the mixing together of natural substances:*

 YOU FOUR, FAITHFUL & TRUTHFUL MINISTERS OF OMNIpotent God, (your Creator) BOZA, OZAB, ZABO, ABOZ, who are in the Southern part of the world, and are powerful and skilled in the mixing together of natural substances: I, John Dee, devoted servant of the same, our Creator, and through the omnipotence of the same, our Creator, and through this mystical Name of our God, EBOZA, humbly require, and vehemently petition, from you, one and all, that at whatever time of my future life that I invoke or call your name, through this mystic Name of God, EBOZA, that you will come to me and appear visibly and personably, and deign to be friendly and favourable unto me. I require that you discharge, implement, and make perfect, benignly, plentily, plainly, and perfectly any and all of my petitions concerning the mixing together of natural substances and other natural secrets, which our Creator hath committed to your understanding, intelligence, and disposition and, as it were, appointed you as His officers and ministers. AMEN

Through this Holy and Mystical Name of God

EBOZA

AMEN

✠

| b | O | a | Z | a |
|---|---|---|---|---|
| u | N | n | a | x |
| a | i | 9 | r | a |
| o | r | p | m | n |
| r | s | O | n | i |
| i | z | i | n | r |

*�This is the invitation to the four good angels of the West, who are powerful and learned in the mixing together of natural substances:*

YOU FOUR, FAITHFUL & TRUTHFUL MINISTERS OF OMNI-potent God, (your Creator) TAAD, AADT, ADTA, DTAA, who are in the Western part of the world, and are powerful and skilled in the mixing together of natural substances: I, John Dee, devoted servant of the smae, our Creator, and through the omni-potence of the same, our Creator, and through this mystical Name of our God, ATAAD, humbly require, and vehemently petition, from you, one and all, that at whatever time of my future life that I invoke or call your name, through this mystic Name of God, ATAAD, that you will come to me and appear visibly and personally, and deign to be friendly and favourable unto me. I require that you discharge, implement, and make perfect, benignly, plentily, plainly, and perfectly any and all of my petitions concerning the mixing together of natural substances and other natural secrets, which our Creator hath committed to your understanding, intelligence, and disposition, and, as it were, appointed you as his officers and ministers. AMEN

Through this Holy and Mystical Name of God
ATAAD
AMEN
✠

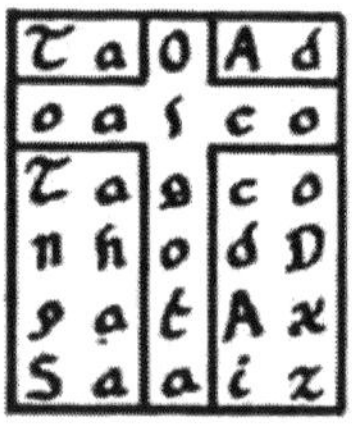

| T | a | 0 | A | d |
|---|---|---|---|---|
| o | a | ſ | c | o |
| T | a | ꝯ | c | o |
| n | h | o | d | D |
| ꝯ | a | t | A | x |
| S | a | a | i | z |

*This is the invitation to the four good angels of the North, who are powerful and learned in the mixing together of natural substances:*

YOU FOUR, FAITHFUL & TRUTHFUL MINISTERS OF OMNI-potent God, (your Creator) DOPA, OPAD, PADO, ADOP, who are in the Northern part of the world, and are powerful and skilled in the mixing together of natural substances: I, John Dee, devoted servant of the same, our Creator, and through the omni-potence of the same, our Creator, and through this mystical Name of our God, ADOPA, humbly require, and vehemently petition, from you, one and all, that at whatever time of my future life that I invoke or call your name, through this mystic Name of God, ADOPA, that you will come to me and appear visibly and personably, and deign to be friendly and favourable unto me. I require that you discharge, implement, and make perfect, benignly, plentily, plainly, and perfectly any and all of my petitions concerning the mixing together of natural substances and other natural secrets, which our Creator hath committed to your understanding, intelligence, and disposition and, as it were, appointed you as His officers and ministers. AMEN

Through this Holy and Mystical Name of God

ADOPA

AMEN

✠

| d | o | n | p | a |
|---|---|---|---|---|
| o | ſ | o | a | G |
| O | P | a | m | n |
| a | p | ſ | s | T |
| s | c | m | i | o |
| V | a | r | s | G |

## CHAPTER XI

# THE ANGELS OF TRANSPORTATION

℣

*These are the sixteen good angels who are powerful in transporting from place to place.**

| QUARTER | GOD NAME | ANGELS | LETTER OF THE CROSS |
|---------|----------|--------|---------------------|
| East | EVTPA | VPTA | L |
| | | TPAV | |
| | | PAVT | |
| | | AVTP | |
| South | EPHRA | PHRA | A |
| | | HRAP | |
| | | RAPH | |
| | | APHR | |
| West | ATDIM | TDIM | N |
| | | DIMT | |
| | | IMTD | |
| | | MTDI | |
| North | AANAA | ANAA | V |
| | | NAAA | |
| | | AAAN | |
| | | AANA | |

* In Locali Mutatione

L

*⚓ This is the invitation to the four good angels of the East, who are powerful in transporting from place to place:*

**O** YOU FOUR FAITHFUL & NOBLE ANGELS & MINISTERS OF our Omnipotent Creator, O VTPA, TPAV, PAVT, & AVTP, who rule uniquely in the Eastern part of the world and whom our Creator has provided and given the skill, strength, and power to be able to transport or transfer any man or thing from one place to another, without injury, harm, offence, or damnation to that man or thing, whether the transference is near or far: I, John Dee, humble and devoted servant of the Omnipotent God, our Creator, through the Reverent Majesty of the same God, our Creator, and through this divine and mystical Name, EVTPA, I humbly require and vehemently petition you, one and all, that whatever future time of my life that I call or invoke you through the Name of God, EVTPA, that you come benignly and peacefully, and appear visibly and personally to me and that you deign to be friendly and favourable to me. I require that you discharge, implement, and make perfect, goodly, truly, plentily, and perfectly, each and every one of my petitions, past and future, concerning local motion, transporting from place to place and any other secrets which you were uniquely conceded and committed the authority and disposition by our God, to His praise, honour, and glory. AMEN

Through this mystical Name of God

EVTPA

AMEN

☩

| u | t | ſ | ƿ | a |
|---|---|---|---|---|
| ƿ | a | L | a | m |
| o | Y | a | u | ƀ |
| P | a | c | o | C |
| r | ƀ | x | n | h |
| d | l | a | r | i |

*This is the invitation to the four good angels of the South, who are powerful in transporting from place to place:*

YOU FOUR FAITHFUL & NOBLE ANGELS & MINISTERS OF our Omnipotent Creator, O PHRA, HRAP, RUPH, and APHR, who rule uniquely in the Southern part of the world and whom our Creator has provided and given the skill, strength, and power to be able to transport or transfer any man or thing from one place to another, without injury, harm, offence or damnation to that man or thing, whether the transference is near or far: I, John Dee, humble and devoted servant of the Omnipotent God our Creator, through the Reverent Majesty of the same God, our Creator, & through this divine and mystical Name, EPHRA, I humbly require and vehemently petition you, one and all, that whatever future time of my life that I call or invoke you through the Name of God, EPHRA, that you come benignly and peacefully, and appear visibly and personally to me and that you deign to be friendly and favourable to me. I require that you discharge, implement, and make perfect, goodly, truly, plentily, and perfectly, each and every one of my petitions, past and future, concerning local motion, transporting from place to place and any other secrets which you were uniquely conceded and committed the authority and disposition by our God, to His praise, honour, and glory. AMEN

Through this mystical Name of God

EPHRA

AMEN

✠

| p | h | a | R | a |
|---|---|---|---|---|
| S | o | n | ɗ | n |
| o | m | a | 9 | 9 |
| 9 | b | e | a | ſ |
| r | ſ | c | m | ✕ |
| ì | a | M | h | ſ |

*This is the invitation to the four good angels of the West, who are powerful in transporting from place to place:*

YOU FOUR FAITHFUL & NOBLE ANGELS & MINISTERS OF our Omnipotent Creator, O TDIM, DIMT, IMTD, and MTDI, who rule uniquely in the Western part of the world and whom our Creator has provided and given the skill, strength, and power to be able to transport or transfer any man or thing from one place to another, without injury, harm, offence, or damnation to that man or thing, whether the transference is near or far: I, John Dee, humble and devoted servant of the Omnipotent God, our Creator, through the Reverent Majesty of the same God, our Creator, and through this divine and mystical Name, ATDIM, I humbly require and vehemently petition you, one and all, that whatever future time of my life that I call or invoke you through the Name of God, ATDIM, that you come benignly and peacefully, and appear visibly and personally to me and that you deign to be friendly and favourable to me. I require that you discharge, implement, and make perfect, goodly, truly, plentily, and perfectly, each and every one of my petitions, past and future, concerning local motion, transporting from place to place and any other secrets which you were uniquely conceded and committed the authority and disposition by our God, to His praise, honour, and glory. AMEN

Through this mystical Name of God

ATDIM

AMEN

✠

| t | D | n | i | m |
|---|---|---|---|---|
| o | m | e | 6 | 6 |
| m | a | ſ | G | m |
| ſ | e | a | o | c |
| V | s | P | s | H |
| r | V | r | o | i |

*⅜This is the invitation to the four good angels of the North, who are powerful in transporting from place to place:*

 YOU FOUR FAITHFUL & NOBLE ANGELS & MINISTERS OF our Omnipotent Creator, O ANAA, NAAA, AAAN, and AANA, who rule uniquely in the Northern part of the world and whom our Creator has provided and given the skill, strength, and power to be able to transport or transfer any man or thing from one place to another, without injury, harm, offence or damnation to that man or thing, whether the transference is near or far: I, John Dee, humble and devoted servant of the Omnipotent God, our Creator, through the Reverent Majesty of the same God, our Creator, and through this divine and mystical Name, AANAA, I humbly require and vehemently petition you, one and all, that whatever future time of my life that I call or invoke you through the Name of God, AANAA, that you come benignly and peacefully, and appear visibly and personally to me and that you deign to be friendly and favourable to me. I require that you discharge, implement, and make perfect, goodly, truly, plentily, and perfectly, each and every one of my petitions, past and future, concerning local motion, transporting from place to place and any other secrets which you were uniquely conceded and committed the authority and disposition by our God, to His praise, honour, and glory. AMEN

Through this mystical Name of God
AANAA
AMEN
✠

| a | n | V | a | a |
|---|---|---|---|---|
| o | b | a | u | a |
| G | m | d | n | m |
| e | c | a | o | ℛ |
| A | m | ſ | o | x |
| b | r | i | a | ℛ |

# THE ANGELS OF THE MECHANICAL ARTS

꙳

*These are the names of the sixteen good angels who are skilled and powerful in the Mechanical Arts.*

| QUARTER | GOD NAME | ANGELS | LETTER OF THE CROSS |
|---------|----------|--------|---------------------|
| East | HCNBR | CNBR<br>NBRC<br>BRCN<br>RCNB | A |
| South | HROAN | ROAN<br>OANR<br>ANRO<br>NROA | C |
| West | PMAGL | MAGL<br>AGLM<br>GLMA<br>LMAG | M |
| North | PPSAC | PSAC<br>SACP<br>ACPS<br>CPSA | V |

*⚜This is the invitation to the four good angels of the East , who are skilled and powerful in the Mecahnical Arts:*

YOU FOUR HOLY & TRUTHFUL MINISTERS OF OMNIPOTENT God, our Crearor, CNBR, NBRC, BRCN, and RCNB, who are in the Eastern part of the world, and who hast by our God been charged and committed with His ministry to practice, impart, teach, and communicate perfect skill in all arts mechanical, to the praise, honour, and glory of our God, I, John Dee, the baptized and marked slave of our Creator, faithfully, prudently, and power-fully desiring to be devout, (to the solace and reward of those good men who are of the Elect, but to the shame and confusion of those evil men who are the enemies of our omnipotent God), do humbly require and vehemently petition from all of you, named above, through the omnipotent wisdom of the same, our God and Creator, and through this holy and mystical Name, HCNBR, that at whatever time in the future of my entire life, that I would call you by name or invoke any, each, or all of you through this Name of God, HCNBR, that you immediately come to me and appear to me, benignly, peacefully, personally, and visibly, and that you be friendly and favourable unto me, and that you discharge, implement, and make perfect immediately, truly, plentifully, manifestly, and perfectly any and all of my pet-itions concerning the Arts Mechanical as well as other mechanical conclusions or experiments.

Through this mystical Name of God
HCNBR
AMEN
✠

| c | N | a | b | r |
|---|---|---|---|---|
| O | i | i | i | t |
| A | b | a | m | o |
| N | a | o | c | O |
| o | c | a | n | m |
| S | h | i | a | ſ |

*This is the invitation to the four good angels of the South, who are skilled and powerful in the Mechanical Arts:*

 YOU FOUR HOLY & TRUTHFUL MINISTERS OF OMNIPOTENT God, our Creator, ROAN, OANR, ANRO, and NROA, who are in the Southern part of the world, and who hast by our God been charged and committed with his ministry to practice, impart, teach and communicate perfect skill in all mechanical arts, to the praise, honour, and glory of our God. I, John Dee, the baptized and marked slave of our Creator, faithfully, prudently, and powerfully desiring to be devout, (to the solace and reward of those good men who are of the Elect, but to the shame and confusion of those evil men who are the enemies of our omnipotent God(, do humbly require and vehemently petition from all of you, named above, through the omnipotent wisdom of the same, our God and Creator, and through this holy and mystical Name, HROAN, that at whatever time in the future of my entire life, that I would call you by name or invoke any, each, or all of you through this Name of God, HROAN, that you immediately come to me and appear to me, benignly, peacefully, personally, and visibly, and that you be friendly and favourable unto me, and that you discharge, implement, and make perfect immediately, truly, plentifully, manifestly, and perfectly any and all of my petitions concerning the Arts Mechanical as well as other mechanical conclusions or experiments.

Through this mystical Name of God
HROAN
AMEN
✠

| ʀ | O | c | o | n |
|---|---|---|---|---|
| A | r | б | i | z |
| O | ρ | a | n | a |
| ∂ | O | ſ | o | P |
| ɾ | ӿ | ρ | a | o |
| a | ӿ | t | i | ɾ |

*This is the invitation to the four good angels of the West, who are skilled and powerful in the Mechanical Arts:*

YOU FOUR HOLY & TRUTHFUL MINISTERS OF OMNIPOTENT God, our Creator, MAGL, AGLM, GLMA, and LMAG, who are in the Western part of the world, and who hast by our God been charged and committed with His ministry to practice, impart, teach , and communicate perfect skill in all arts mechanical, to the praise, honour, and glory of our God. I, John Dee, the baptized and marked slave of our Creator, faithfully, prudently, and powerfully desiring to be devout, (to the solace and reward of those good men who are of the Elect, but to the shame and confusion of those evil men who are the enemies of our omnipotent God), do humbly require and vehemently petition from all of you, named above, through the omnipotent wisdom of the same, our God and Creator, and through this holy and mystical Name, PMAGL, that at whatever time in the future of my entire life, that I would call you by name or invoke any, each, or all of you through this Name of God, PMAGL, that you immediately come to me and appear to me, benignly, peacefully, personally, and visibly, and that you be friendly and favourable unto me, and that you discharge, implement, and make perfect immediately, truly, plentifully, manifestly, and perfectly any and all of my petitions concerning the Arts Mechanical as well as other mechanical conclusions or experiments.

Through this mystical Name of God

PMAGL

AMEN

☩

| M | a | m | g | s |
|---|---|---|---|---|
| o | s | a | a | D |
| g | a | L | c | o |
| n | d | a | z | N |
| i | i | d | P | o |
| x | r | i | n | h |

*⁜This is the invitation to the four good angels of the North, who are skilled and powerful in the Mechanical Arts*

YOU FOUR HOLY & TRUTHFUL MINISTERS OF OMNIPOTENT God, our Creator, PSAC, SACP, ACPS, and CPSA, who are in the Northern part of the world, and who hast by our God been charged and committed with His ministry to practice, impart, teach, and communicate perfect skill in all arts mechanical, to the praise, honour, and glory of our God. I, John Dee, the baptized and marked slave of our Creator, faithfully, prudently, and powerfully desiring to be devout, (to the solace and reward of those good men who are of the Elect, but to the shame and confusion of those evil men who are the enemies of our omnipotent God), do humbly require and vehemently petition from all of you, named above, through the omnipotent wisdom of the same, our God and Creator, and through this holy and mystical Name, PPSAC, that at whatever time in the future of my entire life, that I would call you by name or invoke any, each, or all of you through this Name of God, PPSAC, that you immediately come to me and appear to me, benignly, peacefully, personally, and visibly, and that you be friendly and favourable unto me, and that you discharge, implement, and make perfect immediately, truly, plentifully, manifestly, and perfectly any and all of my petitions concerning the Arts Mechanical as well as other mechanical conclusions or experiments.

Through this mystical Name of God

PPSAC

AMEN

✟

| p | s | u | a | c |
|---|---|---|---|---|
| S | i | o | d | a |
| d | a | ſ | t | Z |
| d | i | x | o | m |
| O | o | D | p | z |
| r | g | o | a | n |

# THE ANGELS OF SECRET DISCOVERY

✿

*These are the names of the sixteen good angels who are skilled and powerful in the discovering the secrets of all men.*

| QUARTER | GOD NAME | ANGELS | LETTER OF THE CROSS |
|---------|----------|--------|---------------------|
| East | HXGZD | XGZD<br>GZDX<br>ZDXG<br>DXGZ | A |
| South | HIAOM | IAOM<br>AOM<br>OMIA<br>MIAO | S |
| West | PNLRX | NLRX<br>LRXN<br>RXNL<br>XNLR | I |
| North | PZIZA | ZIZA<br>IZAZ<br>ZAZI<br>AZIZ | R |

*This is the invitation to the four good angels of the East, who are skilled and powerful in the discovery of the secrets of men.*

O YOU FOUR WISE & TRUTHFUL ANGELS OF THE OMNIPOTENT God, and ministers of our Creator: O you, XGZD, GZDX, ZDXG, and DXGZ, who dwell in the Eastern part of the world, and whom the same, our God, hath assigned and bestowed the great and special office of discovering and understanding the secrets of men of whatver degree, state or condition. I, John Dee, theu devoted servant of the same God, a careful investigator, but by no means curious of the secret endeavors, acts, and events of any type of man (good or evil) unless it might be necessary for the good of the Christian Republic for me to see, understand, and discover, do humbly require and vehemently petition from you, one and all, through our omniscient God and through this mystical Name HXGZD, that, at whatever time of my future lifeɔ that I should call or invoke any or all of you through the Name of God, HXGZD, that you come to me immediately, benignly, and peacefully, and that you appear to me personally and visibly, and that you discharge, implement, and make perfect, truthfully, plentily, and perfectly, all of my petitions (to be done by one, any, or all of you) concerning the secrets of any men, regardless of state and condition.

Through this holy and mystical Name of God
HXGZD
AMEN
✠

| | | | |
|---|---|---|---|
| x | g | a | z | d |
| a | Y | O | a | i |
| a | C | u | c | a |
| n | y | r | a | C |
| o | t | r | o | i |
| y | m | z | o | x |

*⅜This is the invitation to the four good angels of the South, who are skilled and powerful in the discovery of the secrets of men.*

 YOU FOUR WISE & TRUTHFUL ANGELS OF THE OMNIPOTENT God, and ministers of our Creator: O you, IAOM, AOMI, OMIA, and MIAO, who dwell in the Southern part of the world, and whom the same, our God, hath assigned and bestowed the great and special office of discovering and understanding the secrets of men of whatever degree, state, or condition. I, John Dee, the devoted servant of the same God, a careful investigator, but by no means curious of the secret endeavors, acts, and events of any type of man (good or evil) unless it might be necessary for the good of the Christian Republic for me to see, understand, and discover, do humbly require and vehemently petition from you, one and all, through our omniscient God and through this mystical name, HIAOM, that, at whatever time of my future life that I should call or invoke any or all of you through the Name of God, HIAOM, that you come immediately, benignly, and peacefully, and that you appear to me personally and visibly, and that you discharge, implement, and make perfect, truthfully, plentily, and perfectly, all of my petitions (to be done by one, any, of all or you) concerning the secrets of any men, regardless of state and condition.

Through this holy and mystical Name of God
HIAOM
AMEN
☩

| i | a | s | o | m |
|---|---|---|---|---|
| i | f | p | i | z |
| m | S | m | a | L |
| i | a | n | b | a |
| i | z | i | æ | p |
| s | t | r | i | m |

*This is the invitation to the four good angels of the West, who are skilled and powerful in the discovery of the secrets of men.*

 YOU FOUR WISE & TRUTHFUL ANGELS OF THE OMNIPOTENT God, and ministers of our Creator: O you, NLRX, LRXN, RXNL, and XNLR, who dwell in the Western part of the world, and whom the same, our God, hath assigned and bestowed the great and special office of discovering and understanding the secrets of men of whaever degree, state, or conditon. I, John Dee, the devoted servant of the same God, a careful investigator, but by no means curious of the secret endeavors, acts, and events of any type of man (good or evil) unless it might be necessary for the good of the Christian Republic for me to see, understand, and discover, do humbly require and vehemently petition from you, one and all, through our omniscient God and through this mystical Name, PNLRX, that, at whatever time of my future life that I should call or invoke any or all of you through the Name of God, PNLRX, that you come to me immediately, benignly, and peacefully, and that you appear to me personally and visibly, and that you discharge, implement and make perfect, truthfully, plentily, and perfectly, all of my petitions (to be done by one, any, or all of you) concerning the secrets of any men, regardless of state and condition.

Through this holy and mystical Name of God
PNLRX
AMEN
☩

| n | L | i | r | x |
|---|---|---|---|---|
| a | ℒ | a | ℘ | a |
| x | P | a | c | n |
| V | a | a | s | a |
| d | A | s | ℘ | i |
| r | n | d | i | ⅃ |

*⚜This is the invitation to the four good angels of the North, who are skilled and powerful in the discovery of the secrets of men.*

 YOU FOUR WISE & TRUTHFUL ANGELS OF THE OMNIPOTENT God, and ministers of our Creator: O you, ZIZA, IZAZ, ZAZI, and AZIZ, who dwell in the Northern part of the world, and whom the same, our God, hath assigned and bestowed the great and special office of discovering and understanding the secrets of men of whatever degree, state, or condition. I, John Dee, the devoted servant of the same God, a careful investigator, but by no means curious of the secret endeavors, acts, and events of any type of man (good or evil) unless it might be necessary for the good of the Christian Republic for me to see, understand, and discover, do humbly require and vehemently petition from you, one and all, through our omniscient God and through this mystical Name, PZIZA, that, at whatever time of my future life that I should call or invoke any or all of you through the Name of God, PZIZA, that you come to me immediately, benignly, and peacefully, and that you appear to me personally and visibly, and that you discharge, implement, and make perfect, truthfully, plentily, and perfectly, all of my petitions (to be done by one, any, or all of you) concerning the secrets of any men, regardless of state and condition.

Through this holy and mystical Name of God
PZIZA
AMEN
✠

| Z | i | r | Z | a |
|---|---|---|---|---|
| n | r | z | ʃ | m |
| a | d | i | r | e |
| s | i | o | s | p |
| p | a | n | ʃ | i |
| A | c | r | a | r |

FIN

☿ ☿ ☿
☿ ☿
☿

M

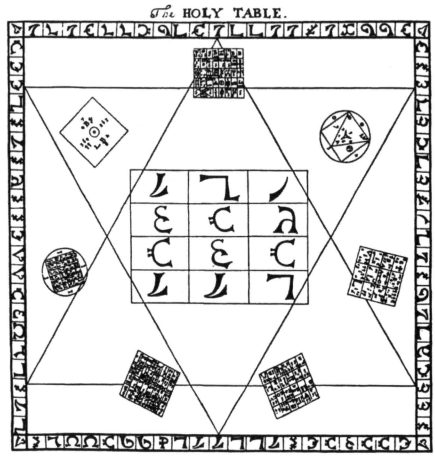

*The* HOLY TABLE.

[*Vide* page 181, ([IJ., number 6.]

# APPENDICES

## Appendix A

## THE PRACTICE OF ENOCHIAN EVOCATION

**T**HERE ARE NO DESCRIPTIONS IN DEE'S EXTANT DIARIES OF actual Enochian evocation rituals, a fact that has led some scholars to conclude that he never attempted the magic. The existence, however, of artifacts such as the wax sigils of Æmeth in the British museum indicate that Dee, at the very least, constructed some of the requisite furniture. In addition, Dee compiled Sloane MS. 3191 (the primary source for *The Enochian Evocation*) to be a working collection of conjurations for use in magical ceremonies. Although it is possible that Dee never went through with the experiments, it is far more likely that he recorded the events in a separate diary that has not survived. Dee was a rabid diarist, and kept at least three concurrent diaries during the period that he was working with Kelly, each diary covering a different aspect of his life. It would be well in character for Dee to initiate a special diary for the practice of the 'radical truths' that he had sought for so many years.

There are many clues that assist in uncovering the operative portions of this arcane branch of magical lore. Sloane MS. 3191, for example , delineates the portions of Enochian evocation that Dee thought were most essential. Other clues are scattered throughout the surviving diaries. Dee describes many scrying sessions, and it is unlikely that the Enochian rituals differed very greatly from those he practiced with his scryers. In addition, many passages from the scrying sessions contain hints and instructions concerning Enochian evocation. Another valuable source of information is the body of magical literature that was available to Dee and Kelly. The effect of Agrippa, for example, upon Dee's philosophical outlook is obvious, and many aspects of Enochian evocation are dependant upon the world-view of

179

the renaissance Magi. Also, Kelly's involvement in black magic indicates influence from other magical texts. When all these sources of information are gathered together, a coherent picture emerges of the practice of Enochian evocation.

This appendix discusses:

1. The personnel & apparel required for the rituals.
2. The furniture and construction of the temple.
3. The book of prayers & conjurations.
4. The Angelic hierarchies
5. The talismans for the Angelic hierarchies.
6. The scheduling of the ceremonies.

### ❡ I. PERSONNEL

ENOCHIAN rituals were practiced by two people, a Magus and Scryer. The Magus chanted the conjurations, compelling the Angels (by the power of the Names of God) to appear within the crystal stone. The Scryer gazed into the crystal and related his visions. The Magus doubled as scribe, recording the visions and the results of the ceremony.

Both Scryer and Magus were expected to lead holy lives (at least while practicing the magic), to cultivate piety and humility, and to abstain from the practice of black magic. During the ceremonies, both were dressed in white linen robes, and the magus wore a magical ring with a gold seal (as shown in Book Two). Other renaissance magical texts recommend that the Magus wear a crown and carry a magical wand and or sword, but none of these are mentioned in Dee's work.

### ❡ II. FURNITURE

BEFORE practicing Enochian evocation, the Magus and Scryer located or constructed the following items:

1. A crystal ball. This was handled only by the magus or the scryer. Dee's was rather small, about two inches in diameter.
2. A circular wax tablet, 9 inches in diameter and 1.5 inches thick, inscribed on the front with the sigil of Æmeth and on the back with a cross. These designs are shown in Book Two. The center of the front was hollowed out slightly, so that

the crystal ball could easily be placed on top of the Sigil.

3. Four wax tablets, about 4 inches in diameter, similarly inscribed.

4. A red silk 'rug', two yards square.

5. A red and green (or multi-coloured) tablecloth, about 1.5 yards square, with tassles at each corner.

6. A table constructed of 'sweet wood' [cedar?] a yard (two cubits) square, with yard long legs. Each leg terminated with a hollow cylinder, slightly more than 4 inches on the inside diameter and about 0.5 inches thick. The basic structure of this table is shown in Book Two; because of its low profile, two wooden stools were probably also necessary. A set of elaborate sigils were to be painted in yellow oils on the top surface of the table. The arrangement of these sigils is too complex to be reproduced in this volume, but can be found in *The True Relation* between the Preface and the first book, on the page labeled 'The Holy Table'.

7. Twelve banners or flags each embroidered with a Name of God as shown in Book Five.

This furniture was arranged into a temple where Enochian evocation could be practiced. This may have been intended to be in the open air rather than within a building, as there are no descriptions of candles or torches. Furthermore, the magical circle specifies 'Terra' [Earth], which may or may not have been intended symbolically.

The temple was constructed in the following manner:

1. The place of working was enclosed by a circle as shown in Book Five, Chapter Three. The banners were propped at the circle's edge.

2. The red silk rug was laid in the center of the circle.

3. The four small wax tablets were arranged in a square pattern in the center of the silk rug, 1 yard square.

4. The table was balanced upon the wax tablets, so that the hollow cylinders at the end of the table legs overlapped them.

5. The large wax tablet was placed on the center of the table.

6. The silk tablecloth was draped over the table, covering the large wax tablet, so that the tassles dangled almost to the floor.

7. The crystal was laid on the top of the tablecloth, balanced on the indentation in the wax tablet.

## ¶ III. The Magical Book

The Magus was required to have a book in which prayers and conjurations were recorded for use within the temple. For the complete practice of Enochian evocation, it probably would have had the following contents:

### §1: Prayers

The Oration to God—as shown in Book Two, Chapter Five.

The Prayer of Enoch—as shown in Book One, Chapter Two.

The Fundamental Obesance—as shown in Book Five, Chapter Four.

### §2. Conjurations

The Heptarchic Conjurations—formed by inserting the specific attributes of each King and Prince (as shown in Book Two, Chapter Seven) with the generalized conjuration (as shown in Book Two, Chapter Six).

The Angelical Keys—as shown in Book Three. These were to be written in both Angelical and English. Note that the last key was to be repeated 30 times, with the third word altered to indicate the Aire being worked. In Sloane MS. 3191, the the various Aires are listed in the margin. The individual names of the Aires are given in Book Four, Column Four.

The Invitations to the Angels of the Quarters—as shown in Book Five, Chapters Five through Thirteen.

The ordering of Dee's workbooks suggests that he intended a certain cross-semination of the earlier (Heptarchic) and later (Angelical) systems. In any case, the magical book is described in Dee's diaries as consisting *first of the invocation of the Names of God and second of the invocation of the Angels, by the Names of God*—an ordering is preserved in the contents above.

Note that, unlike other renaissance magical systems, Enochian evocation does not include a 'Dismissal' or 'Licence to Depart', a conjuration designed to send a spirit back to its dwelling place. Dee evidently felt this to be unnecessary, although most renaissance Magi would have considered this omission dangerous.

**¶ IV. THE ANGELS**

ENOCHIAN evocation was believed to summon three interrelated hierarchies of angels:

1. THE HEPTARCHICAL ROYALTY—who were believed to govern *all earthly actions, & disperse of the will of the Creator.* One conjured them to obtain *knowledge of God truly, the number and doings of His Angels perfectly and the beginning and ending of Nature substantially.* These Angels were based upon the 7 planets and the 7 days of the week.

2. THE ANGELS OF THE AIRES—who were believed to rule over the various countries of the earth. One conjured them to *subvert whole countries without armies, to get the favour of all the* (human) *Princes, & to know the secret treasure of the waters, and the unknown caves of the earth.* These Angels were based on the 12 houses of the Zodiac and the 30 Aires, which were evidently subdivisions of the 'vault of stars' in which the 'fixed stars' were believed to reside.

3. THE ANGELS OF THE QUARTERS—who were believed to have been *put onto the earth so that the Devil's envious will might be bridled, the determinations of God fulfilled, and his creatures kept and preserved.* One conjured them to obtain a variety of semi-divine powers and capabilities. These Angels were based upon the 4 Elements and the 4 compass points.

Thus Enochian evocation consisted of a complete panoply of magical art, covering planetary, zodiacal, and elemental operations and reputed to control hundreds of named and thousands of unnamed Angelic creatures. Because of the complexity of these Angelic hierarchies, I shall discuss each in detail.

§1. THE HEPTARCHICAL ROYALTY

THE HEPTARCHICAL Royalty are described in Book Two, Chapter Four, and were believed to rule over the days of the week and the planets. The relationship of the primary Heptarchical hierarchy is shown in the following figure·

## KING CARMARA

### PRINCE HAGONEL

| | | | | | | | |
|---|---|---|---|---|---|---|---|
| Sons of Light | I | Ih | Isr | Dmal | Hecoa | Beigia | Stimcul |
| Sons of the Sons of Light | EL | An | Ave | Liba | Rocle | Hagonel | Ilemese |
| Kings | BALIGON | BNASPOL | BOBOGEL | BABALEL | BYNEPOR | BNAPSEN | BLUMAZA |
| Princes | BAGANOL | BLISDON | BORNOGO | BEFAFES | BUTMONO | BRORGES | BRALGES |

| The Table of the 42 Ministers | | | | | | |
|---|---|---|---|---|---|---|
| AOAYNNL | ELGNSEB | LEENARB | EILOMFO | BBARNFL | BANSSZE | OESNGLE |
| LBBNAAV | NLINZVB | LNANAEB | NEOTPTA | BBAIGAO | BYAPARE | AVZNILN |
| IOAESPM | SFAMLLB | ROEMNAB | SAGACIY | BBALPAE | BNAMGEN | YLLMAFS |
| GGLPPSA | OOGOSRS | LEAORIB | ONEDPON | BBANIFG | BNVAGES | NRSOGOO |
| OEEOOEZ | NRPCRRB | NEICIAB | NOONMAN | BBOSNIA | BLBOPOO | NRRCPRN |
| NLLRLNA | ergdbab | AOIDIAB | ETEVLGL | BBASNOD | BABEPEN | LABDGRB |
| (Fri.) | (Wed.) | (Sun.) | (Tues.), | (Thurs.) | (Sat.) | (Mon.) |

Note that the 'Son of the Sons' HAGONEL had a different sigil than PRINCE HAGONEL and thus was a different angelic personage.

The names of the 42 ministers were generated from the each table by starting with each letter and continuing rightwards to the end of the table, then looping around to the beginning. This made six sets of seven ministers per day, each set ruling for four hours [beginning at midnight]. For example, the 42 ministers for Prince BAGANOL (Friday) are

| | | | | | | | |
|---|---|---|---|---|---|---|---|
| 12AM— 4AM | Aoaynnl | Oaynnla | Aynnlao | Ynnlaoa | Nnlaoay | Nlaoayn | Laoaynn |
| 4AM— 8AM | Lbbnaav | Bbnaavl | Bnaavlb | Naavlbb | Aavlbbn | Avlbbna | vlbbnaa |
| 8AM—12PM | Ioæspm | Oæspmi | Aespmio | Espmioa | spmioæ | Pmioæs | Mioæsp |
| 12PM— 4PM | Gglppsa | Glppsag | Lppsagg | Ppsaggl | Psagglp | Sagglpp | Agglpps |
| 4PM— 8PM | Oeeooez | Eeooezo | Eooezoe | Ooezoee | Oezoeeo | Ezoeeoo | Zoeeooe |
| 8PM—12AM | Nllrlna | Llrlnan | Lrlnanl | Rlnanll | Lnanllr | Nanllrl | Anllrln |

The Heptarchical Royalty also included a set of 49 planetary angels, of whom 14 were the Kings and Princes for the days. The 'Table of the 49 Good Angels' at the close of Book Two shows the primary planetary attribution of each of these entities. Curiously, the planetary attributions of the Kings were the only ones that matched the traditional linking of the days of the week with the planets. By extrapolation, it is likely that each angel had a double attribution as follows:

| SUNDAY | | MONDAY | |
|---|---|---|---|
| BOBOGEL | Sol of Sol | BLUMAZA | Luna of Luna |
| BORNOGO | Sol of Venus | BRALGES | Luna of Saturn |
| Bablibo | Sol of Luna | Baspalo | Luna of Mercury |
| Buscnab | Sol of Saturn | Belmara | Luna of Jupiter |
| Bariges | Sol of Mercury | Bragiop | Luna of Mars |
| Barnafa | Sol of Jupiter | Brisfli | Luna of Sol |
| Bonefon | Sol of Mars | Basledf | Luna of Venus |

| TUESDAY | | WEDNESDAY | |
|---|---|---|---|
| BABALEL | Mars of Mars | BNASPOL | Mercury of Mrcry |
| BEFAFES | Mars of Sol | BLISDON | Mercury of Jupitr |
| Bapnido | Mars of Venus | Bazpama | Mercury of Mars |
| Busduna | Mars of Luna | Bernole | Mercury of Sol |
| Bminpol | Mars of Saturn | Blamapo | Mercury of Venus |
| Binofon | Mars of Mercury | Barfort | Mercury of Luna |
| Bmilges | Mars of Jupiter | Bliigan | Mercury of Satur |

| THURSDAY | | FRIDAY | |
|---|---|---|---|
| BYNEPOR | Jupiter of Jupiter | BALIGON | Venus of Venus |
| BUTMONO | Jupiter of Mars | BAGENOL | Venus of Luna |
| Basmelo | Jupiter of Sol | Bormifa | Venus of Saturn |
| Besgeme | Jupiter of Venus | Binodab | Venus of Mercury |
| Blingef | Jupiter of Luna | Benpagi | Venus of Jupiter |
| Bartiro | Jupiter of Saturn | Bermale | Venus of Mars |
| Baldago | Jupiter of Merc. | Bagnole | Venus of Sol |

SATURDAY

| BNAPSEN | Saturn of Saturn |
| BRORGES | Saturn of Mercury |
| Balceor | Saturn of Jupiter |
| Blintom | Saturn of Mars |
| Branglo | Saturn of Sol |
| Bmamgal | Saturn of Venus |
| Bamnode | Saturn of Luna |

## §2. THE ANGELS OF THE AIRES

THE 91 PRINCIPAL Angels of the Aires are listed in tabular form in Book Four.

COLUMN ONE gives the name of the country over which each Angel rules. These are based on Ptolemy's Geography.

COLUMN TWO gives the name of each Angel, which is the same as the name of the part of the Earth as imposed by God.

COLUMN THREE gives the sigil for each Angel. These are derived from the Great Table of the Quarters, by connecting the letters that spell the Angel's name. Note that 'PARAOAN' is an 'overlay' using letters belonging to other Angels, (beginning with the 'P' in PARZIBA) and that 'LEXARPH', 'COMANAN', and 'TABITOM' are generated from the central cross. 'LEXARPH uses the 'L' at the bottom right corner of the Western quarter. These sigils are not given in Sloane MS. 3191, but are included here for completeness. Note also that a sigil is given in the table for an entity LAXDIZI, which is not in the 91 Aires.

COLUMN FOUR gives the Aire in which the Angel dwells. These are evidently similar to the layers of Heaven described in Gnostic texts. The order LIL is the highest and TEX is the lowest; note that the Holy Land is governed by LIL.

COLUMN FIVE gives the number of servitor Angels (ministers) that are controlled by each Angel.

COLUMN SIX gives the total of all the Angels ruling in each Aire.

COLUMN SEVEN gives the names of the Angelic Kings that rule over each Angel. There is one King per sign of the Zodiac: 1. OLPAGED for Scorpio, 2. ZIRACAH for Aquarius, 3. HONONOL for Leo, 4. ZARNAAH for Gemini, 5. GEBABAL for Libra, 6. ZURCHOL for Pisces, 7. ALPUDUS for Cancer, 8. CADDAMP for Sagittarius, 9. ZARZILG for Virgo, 10. LAVAVOTH for Aries, 11. ZINGGEN for Capricorn & 12. ARFALOG for Taurus.

COLUMN EIGHT gives the tribe of Israel that corresponds to the Angelic King and each sign of the Zodiac.

COLUMN NINE gives the compass points that should be faced when invoking each angel.

§3. THE ANGELS OF THE QUARTERS

THE ANGELS of the Quarters are listed in detail at the beginning of Chapters Five through Thirteen of Book Five. A cursory examination of the crosses on the tables accompaning each 'Invitation' [conjuration] reveals how these names are generated. Many of the Angels have dual names—presumably both are correct, as both are used in the invitations.

The names of the cacodemons in Chapters Six through Nine are generated by taking a letter from the central cross of the Great Table, and combining it with the first two letters of each Angel's name. For example, the cacodemon Xcz is formed by taking the 'X' in EXARP and combining it with the 'Cz' in CZNS or CZONS. These cacodemons are the only vestige of black magic in Dee's evocation system, other than the stipulation that the word VAOAN in the first Angelical key is to be altered to VOOAN when conjuring evil spirits.

€ V. TALISMANS

THE USE of various talismans were considered necessary for the practice of evocation magic in general, and were probably used for Enochian evocation as well. Only one Enochian talisman has survived: a beautiful gold disk in the British Museum. *A True Relation* shows an engraving of his disk on page preceding THE HOLY TABLE; the talisman commemorates a vision that Kelly had of the Angels of the Quarters:

*A Vision. The sign of the love of God toward his faithful. Four sumptuous and belligerant Castles, out of the which sounded Trumpets thrice.*

*⚔ The sign of Majesty, the Cloth of the passage was cast forth.*

*⚔ In the East, the cloth red; after the new smitten blood*

*⚔ In the South, the cloth white, Lilly-colour*

*⚔ In the West a cloth, the skins of many Dragons, green; garlic bladed.*

*⚔ In the North, the cloth, Hair-coloured, Bilbery juyce.*

*The Trumpets sound once. The gates open. The four Castles are moved. There issueth 4 Trumpeters, whose Trumpets are a Pyramis, six cones, wreathed. There followeth out of every Castle 3, holding up their Banners displayed, with ensigne, the Names of God. There follow Seniors six, alike from the four Gates: After them cometh from every part a King: whose Princes are five, gardant, and holding up his train. Next issueth the Crosse of 4 angels, of the Majesty of Creation in God attended upon everyone, with 4: a white Cloud, 4 Crosses, bearing the witnesses of the Covenant of God, with the Prince gone out before; which were confirmed, everyone, with ten Angels, visible in countenance; After every Crosses, attendeth 16 Angels, dispositors of the will of those, that govern the Castles. They proceed. And, in and about the middle of the Court, the Ensigns keep their standings, opposite to the middle of the Gate: The rest pause. The 24 Senators meet: They seem to consult. It vanisheth.*

Although the use for the gold disk is not known, it may have been worn as a protective amulet during the Enochian evocation ritual

The Magus was definitely required to construct a talisman for each group of Angels that he wished to conjure. These were made of 'sweet wood', with the characters 'painted' upon them. The talismans were *held in the hand as thou shalt have cause to use them*, implying that the Magus held them during the prayers. During the conjurations, however, *thy feet must be placed upon these tables*, indicating that the Magus' dominance over the Angels was signified by his standing upon the Talisman.

Although none of these talismans appear to have survived, the talismanic methods of Agrippa can be applied to devise probable reconstructions of these important ceremonial objects.

§1. TALISMANS FOR THE HEPTARCHICAL ROYALTY

ALTHOUGH this hierarchy includes several hundred entities, only the prince of each day and the SONS OF THE SONS OF LIGHT actually have their own 'signatures' or sigils. Evidently this means that a single talisman was to be constructed for each day, with an extra one for King CARMARA and Prince HAGONEL. The following sample represents a speculative reconstruction of the talisman for the conjuration of the Angels of Friday:

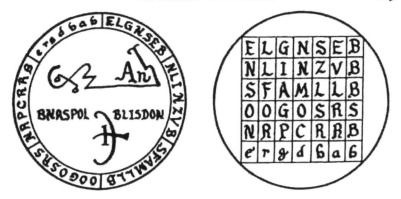

## §2. TALISMANS FOR THE ANGELS OF THE AIRES

EACH OF THE 91 Princes has his [or her] own signature, which clearly implies that 91 separate talismans were to be constructed. The Angelic Kings of the Zodiac have no signatures, which indicates that their name alone (like the magical Names of God) carried the requisite power to invoke their influence. The following sample represents a speculative reconstruction of the talisman for the conjuration of PASCOMB, the Earthly Guardian of Syria:

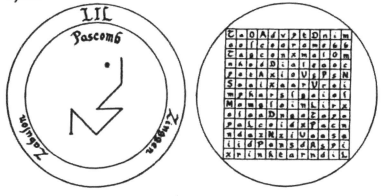

## §3. TALISMANS FOR THE ANGELS OF THE QUARTERS

NONE OF THE Angels of the Quarters have their own signatures, a fact that would seem to indicate the relatively exalted status of these entities. The following sample represents a speculative reconstruction of the talisman for the conjuration of the Angels of Transformation that dwell in the West:

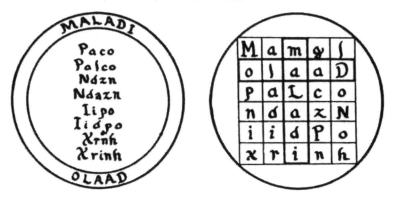

### §4. ENOCHIAN LETTERS

IT IS POSSIBLE that, rather than Roman letters, the 'Enochian' alphabet was to be used to draw up the talismans (although no Enochian letters appear in Sloane MS. 3191). There are several versions of this magical alphabet in Dee's diaries; the following version appears to be a script rendition, as it is much easier to write with a quill pen than the sigil-like letters that appear later in Dee's notes.

❡ VI. THE CEREMONIES

AFTER THE FURNITURE, book, and talisman had been prepared, the following schedule was to be kept:

1. FIRST FOUR DAYS—prayers were fervently spoken three times daily.
2. NEXT FOURTEEN DAYS—while continuing with the prayers, conjurations were added to the agenda.
3. THE FIFTEENTH DAY—at this point the prayers and conjurations were believed to become effective, and the Angels were supposed to appear within the crystal.

Once the Angels had appeared, it was no longer considered necessary to go through the entire repetory to conjure them. Once successfully conjured, the Angels were to remain obedient to the Magus for the remainder of his life.

It is probable that some cross-semination might have been intended, for example, using the first 18 Keys as preliminary conjurations to summoning the Angels of the Quarters. Dee also tended to punctuate his scrying sessions with readings from the Bible; *Psalm* 33 is mentioned specifically.

## Appendix B

# TRANSLATOR'S NOTES

### *The Story of the Manuscripts*

**T**HE SURVIVAL OF THE MAGICAL MANUSCRIPTS OF JOHN DEE was an accident, or more accurately, a series of accidents and coincidences that rival in strangeness the subject matter that the manuscripts contain.

Even while they were being written, certain of the most essential manuscripts were almost destroyed. Although the incident and the motivations behind it are not mentioned in any of the extant diaries, Dee describes their reappearance:

> *I espied . . . a sheet of faire white paper lying tossed to and fro in the wind. I rose and went up to it and there I found three of my Books lying, which were so diligently burnt the tenth day of April last. The three books were:* 1. Enoch his Book, 2. The 48 Claves Angelicæ, 3. Liber Scientia terrestris auxilii & victoriæ.*[Additional manuscripts were then discovered to be:] *in the back of the furnace . . . the hole which was not greater than the thickness of a brick.*†

Perhaps to prevent further mishaps, Dee later secreted a number of the more important manuscripts in the false bottom of a cedar chest, *whose lock and hinges [were] extraordinarily neat,* where they remained hidden for over 50 years. The chest was sold at the auction following Dee's death to one Mr. John Woodall, and eventually found its way into a furniture shop in Adle Street on London. A Mr. Jones, confectioner, bought it for his wife, and for twenty years the chest with its secret treasure remained in her boudoir. Then one day, upon moving the chest, Mrs. Jones *heard some loose thing rattle it, toward the right hand end, under the box or till.* Her husband pried open the bottom, revealing a *private drawer, which being drawn out, therein were found diverse books*

---

\* Casaubon, *op. cit.,* p. 418.
† *Ibidem,* p. 419.

*in manuscript and papers, together with a little box, and therein a chaplet of olive beads, and a cross of wood hanging at the end of them.**

Ignorant of the value of the papers, they allowed *their servant maid to waste about one half of them under pies, and other like uses* but later *kept the rest more safe.* Four years later, Mrs. Jones was forced to flee the great fire of London and, *though the chest perished in the flames, because not easily to be removed, yet the books were taken out and carried with the rest of her goods.* She later remarried a Mr. Wale, who identified the manuscripts and transferred them to Elias Ashmole, a respected scholar, for transcription and preservation.†

Elias Ashmole also preserved a number of Dee's diaries (December 22, 1581 to May 23, 1583) that were in the library of one Samuel Story. Yet another 17th Century scholar, Meric Casaubon discovered [and published in the *True Relation*] additional diaries from April 20, 1583 to May 23, 1587 in the library of Sir Thomas Cotton, who had inherited them from his father, Sir Robert Cotton, one of Dee's contemporaries. Casaubon also located a very rare fragment of Dee's diaries from late in his life (March 20, 1607 to September 7, 1607), which had been *underground, God knows how long.*‡

The preservation of Dee's manuscripts by Ashmole & Casaubon illustrates that the importance of Dee's manuscripts was already recognized within 50 years of his death. These manuscripts have had an enormous effect upon the development of occultism in Great Britian and the United States. An interesting fragment, included at the back of Sloane MS.3677 (Ashmole's copy of Sloane MS. 3188), describes the finding of treasure using magical names from the Enochian system. From internal references and style of handwriting, we know that this fragment dates from the mid-17th Century, indicating that the Enochian magical system was maintained in practical use after Dee's death. It is possible that elements of the system may have been introduced into the Rosicrucian teachings by Ashmole; in any case magicians of later centuries have constructed elaborate additions to Dee's original system.

* *Vide*, Ashmole's preface to Sloane MS. 3677.
† *Ibidem.*
‡ *Vide* Casaubon's Preface to the *True Relation.*

N

## GENERAL METHOD OF TRANSLATION
## & TRANSCRIPTION

☿

THE ENTIRE CORPUS of Dee's magical work is far too large to present in a single volume. The *Enochian Evocation* is intended to present the essential core of Dee's evocation system arranged in a fashion similar to other renaissance evocation texts. It was transcribed, translated and edited according to the following procedure:

1. Manuscripts copies were obtained in microfilm from the British Library.
2. The various manuscripts were cross-compared to differentiate between essential and non-essential portions. The first level of cross-comparison was performed at this time.
3. The textual material from the essential portions of the manuscripts was transcribed.
4. Latin portions were translated.
5. The resulting corpus was subjected to further cross-comparison and linguistic analysis, and arranged to resemble a typical evocation text of the renaissance.
6. The text was edited for consistancy and clarity.
7. The various sigils and figures for the text were carefully traced and restored from microfilm prints of the source manuscripts.
8. To clarify discrepancies, I traveled to London and examined Sloane MS. 3191 personally at the British Library.
9. The resulting material was brought to completion and published by Heptangle Books.

### Notes on Book One

BOOK ONE consists of excerpts from four of Dee's diaries, all contained in Cotton Appendix XLVI and published in the *True Relation*:

*Mensis Mysticus Saobaticus Pars primus ejusdem* , op. cit. 73-114
*Libri Mystici Apertorii Cracoviensis Sabbatici*, op. cit., 115-152
*Libri Semptimi Apertorii Cracoviensis Mystici Sabbatici*, op. cit., 153-202
*Libri Cracoviensis Mysticus Apertorius Præteria Præmium Madimianum*, op. cit., 203-212

The intent of Book One is to provide the pseudo-history of the magic as related by Kelly's angels, as well as hints as to its purpose and practice. Nearly every renaissance magical text contains such a 'pedigree', which is entirely lacking in Sloane MS. 3191.

### Notes on Book Two

BOOK TWO consists primarily of *De Heptarchia Mystica*, which is contained in Sloane MS. 3191, 32[ro] to 51[ro]. The sigil of Æmeth, the ring of Solomon, and the table are from *Mysteriorum Liber Primus* in Sloane MS. 3188. The first three chapters of *De Heptarchia Mystica* (as presented in MS. 3191) contain cross-references to dates in Sloane MS. 3188; these have been omitted as unnecessary. Sloane MS. 3677 and Sloane MS. 3678 (Elias Ashmole's copies of MSS. 3188 and 3199 respectively) were also used for additional readings.

### Notes on Book Three

BOOK THREE is based upon the 49 *Claves Angelicæ*, contained in Sloane MS. 3191, 1[ro] to 13[ro]. Because so many versions of the Angelical Keys have been published in the past, I have taken a different approach in the present volume.

The first column of Book Three contains a cross-reference number for each Angelical word, showing the key that it is in, as well as its numerical position in that key. The second column shows a corrected version of the Enochian, the result of extensive cross-comparison and linguistic analysis. Corrections based upon

Nn

Cotton Appendix xlvi have been incorporated, as well as simple corrections based on common-sense grammatical rules. Variants from Sloane ms. 3191 reading have been documented in footnotes, except where the correction was sufficiently obvious.§ Presumably an even more self-consistent version of the keys could be generated with further cross analysis. Column 2 represents what I believe to be the logical limit of amendation; further corrections would deviate too greatly from the keys as dictated by Kelly.

Column 3 contains an exact transcription of the Angelical version of the keys in Sloane ms. 3191; the pronunciation marks are Dee's own. Coumn 4 contains an exact transcription of the English version of the keys in Sloane ms. 3191; the punctuation and spelling is Dee's own. Lacunæ in the text are described in the footnotes. Note that Sloane ms. 3191 shows the Angelical left to right, with the English written above. I have returned the format to that used in Cotton Appendix xlvi—a downwardly enumerated matched list.

Additional readings for Book Three were taken from Sloane ms. 3678 (Ashmole's copy of Sloane ms. 3191) and the following books from Sloane ms. 3188:

*Mensis Mysticus Saobaticus Pars primus ejusdem*, Casaubon, *op. cit.* pgs. 73-114

*Libri Mystici Apertorii Cracoviensis Sabbatici, ibid.,* pgs. 115-152.

*Libri Semptimi Apertorii Cracoviensis Mystici Sabbatici, ibid.,* 153-202

*Libri Cracoviensis Mysticus Apertorius Præteria Præmium Madimianum, ibid.,* pgs., 203-212.

*Notes on Book Four*

Book Four is the first part of the *Liber Scientiæ Auxilii et Victoriæ Terrestris*, contained in Sloane ms. 3191, 14[ro] to 31[ro]. The biblical quotes at the beginning refer obviously to the figure showing the ordering of the tribes of Israel. In Sloane ms. 3191, this figure appears on 31[ro]. I have redrawn ir with English captions and inserted it next to the quotes that refer to it. The large table of sigils at the end of Book Four is actually [57vo] & 58[ro] in Sloane ms. 3191; since the sigils refer directly to the

§ An early version of the corrected keys appeared in *Gnostica Magazine* Number 47, September 1978.

third and fourth columns of the lists in Book Four, I have included it here as a bridge into Book Five. These sigils are overlays to the GREAT TABLE in Book Five.

*Notes on Book Five*

BOOK FIVE is taken from the remainder of *Liber Scientia* following *De Heptarchia Mystica* in Sloane MS. 3191, 52[ro] to [80 vo]. The GREAT TABLE (not to be confused with the 'Great Table' published in the preface to the *True Relation*) proposed some interesting transcription problems. Sloane MS. 3191 contains three variants (if you include the sigils shown in Book Four), while two additional variants are given in Cotton Appendix XLVI. Within all the variant tables are corrections, slashed letters, and amendations, indicating a series of changes. The problem lies in that the final version (which wasn't completed until 1587, three years after the original table was dictated) does not match the names of the angels as given in Sloane MS. 3191. I have therefore chosen to give two versions of the table, the first matching the angels, and the second representing the final corrections made in 1587. The intermediary versions I have omitted as unessential. The ambitious scholar is free to retrofit the angelic names to the 'corrected' table, as it is sufficiently obvious how each name is generated from the table.* It should be noted that my presentation of this table as two seperate versions departs significantly from the Golden Dawn tradition of including all the variant letters in each square. I judged this approach as unsatisfactory, because every other 'magic square' in renaissance magic contains only one element per square, and because many of the letters included in the G. D. version are clearly scratched out in the original manuscript. The tables in the present volume represent what I believe to be an accurate portrayal of what Dee and Kelly intended. The breakdown of Book Five into individual chapters is not in Sloane MS. 3191, but the material lends itself well to this approach, as there are distinct sets of tables and conjurations.

---

* *Vide* Israel Regardie, *How to Make and Use Talismans*, New York: Weiser, 1972.

# BIBLIOGRAPHY

## §1. *Manuscripts*

The Sloane and Cotton collections are in the British Library. The Bodeleian and Ashmolean collections are at Oxford.

SLOANE MS. 3191.

This manuscript is the only book of ceremonial magic extant in Dee's handwriting. It consists of three separate 'books,' each detailing a different aspect of Dee's angelic magical system. The books are:—

49 *Claves Angelicæ Anno* 1584 *Cracoviæ* (*Liber* 18) which contains Dee's transcription of the Angelical Keys (often called the the *Enochian Keys* or *Enochian Calls*.

*Liber Scientiæ Auxilii et Victoriæ Terrestris* which contains a complex system of magic based upon the Great Table (often called *The Table of Watchtowers*). It is entirely in Latin, and related to the *Call of the Thirty Aires*.

*De Heptarchia Mystica* which describes a complete system of planetary magic, along with excerpts from the various scrying sessions.

SLOANE MS. 3188.

This manuscript contains Dee's earliest scrying sessions. It contains six individual 'books,' which are:—

*Mysteriorum Liber Primus* covering December 22, 1581 to March 15, 1582, and containing a ceremony with Saul (Dee's first scryer) and the first ceremonies with Edward Talbot, in which the table and Solomon's ring are described.

*Mysteriorum Liber Secundus* covering March 6, 1582 to March 21, 1582, and containin the first elements of the Heptarchic system, the spirits of the Sigil of Æmeth, and the first suggestion that an antediluvian language would be delivered to Dee. The title page is missing, but can be inferred from textual references in Sloane MS. 3677.

*Mysteriorum Liber Tertius* covering April 28, 1582 to May 4, 1582, and containing numerous sigils related but apparently not essential to the Heptarchic system, as well as the names of the 49 good angels.

*Quartus Liber Mysteriorum* covering November 15, 1583 to November 21, 1583, and containing the remainder of the Heptarchic system; this book is the first to record the name of Edward Kelly as the scryer.

*Liber Mysteriorum Quintus* covering March 23, 1583 to April 18, 1583, and containing the tables later transcribed by Kelly into Sloane MS. 3189.

*Quinti Libri Mysteriorum Appendix* covering April 20, 1583 to May 23, 1583, and containing the famous *Enochian* letters, as well as information concerning the construction of the *Great Table*.

COTTON APPENDIX XLVI, PARTS 1 & 2.

This manuscript is occasionally referred to as Royal Appendix XLVI, or Sloane MS. 5007. It contains thirteen 'books,' which are:-

*Liber Mysteriorum (et Sancti) parallelus Novalisque* covering May 28,

1583 to July 4, 1583, and containing the tail end of the Heptarchic system and the only recorded incident of Kelly
speaking Greek.

*Liber Peregrinationis Prime Videlicet A Mortlaco Angeliæ Ad Crac-
oniam Poloniæ* covering September 21, 1583 to March 13,
1584, and containing the journey from Mortlack to Cracow
Poland and various political speculations.

*Mensis Mysticus Saobaticus Pars primus ejusdem* covering April 10,
1584 to April 30, 1584, and containing the dictations of the
first four calls (backwards).

*Libri Mystici Apertorii Cracoviensis Sabbatici* covering May 7, 1584
to May 22, 1584, and containing the remainder of the call
(except for the call of the Thirty aires) in the Angelical
tongue, and the spirits of the Thirty aires.

*Libri Septimi Cracoviensis Mystici Sabbatici* covering May 23, 1584
to July 12, 1584, and containing the geographic locations of
the spirits of the Thirty aires, the *Great Table* or *Watchtowers*,
and the first third of the *Call of the Thirty Aires.*

*Libri Cracoviensis Mysticus Apertorius Præterea Præmium Madimi-
anum* covering July 12, 1584 to August 15, 1584, and containing the remainder of the *Call of the Thirty Aires*, as well
as the names of the Thirty aires.

*Mysteriorum Pragensium Liber Primus Cæsareusque* covering August
15, 1584 to October 8, 1584, and containing an attempt to
convince the Holy Roman Emperor of the canonical nature
of the visions.

*Mysteriorum Pragensium Confirmatio* covering December 20, 1584
to March 20, 1585, and containing mostly political specul-
ation.

*Mysteriorum Cracoveinsium Stephanicorum Mysteria Stephanica* covering April 12, 1585 to June 6, 1585, and containing an alchemical formula and a letter from Dee's wife to the spirits.

*Unica Action, quæ Pucciana vocetor* covering August 6, 1585 to September 6, 1585, and containing religious visions obviously meant to impress the Papal Nuncio who was then attending the ceremonies.

*Liber Resurrectionis Pragæ, Pactum sev Fœdus Sabbatismi* covering fragments from April 30, 1586 to January 21, 1587, and containing further ceremonies with the Papal Nuncio.

*Actio TertiaTrebonæ Generalis* covering April 4, 1587 to May 23, 1587, and containing a complex series of corrections to the *Watch-towers* and the infamous wife-swapping episode.

*Jesus, Omnipotens sempiterne & une Deus* covering March 20, 1607 to September 7, 1607 and containing the last records of Dee's magical experiments.

§2. *Related Manuscripts.*

The following manuscripts are of general interest to the scholar of Dee's magical system:

SLOANE MS. 3677—Elias Ashmole's copy of Sloane MS. 3188.

SLOANE MS. 3678—Elias Ashmole's copy of Sloane MS. 3191.

SLOANE MS. 3189, *Liber Mysteriorum Sextus and Sanctus* or *The Book of Enoch revealed to John Dee by the Angels* which contains 49 double-sided tables of (apparently) random letters. It is in Edward Kelly's handwriting.

SLOANE MS. 2599—Copy of Sloane MS. 3189, possibly by Ashmole.

SLOANE MS. 78—contains fragments of Sloane MS. 3189.

SLOANE MS. 2575—contains fragments of Sloane MS. 3189.

### §3. *More Related Manuscripts.*

I have not personally examined or researched the following manuscripts, but I include their references as points for future study. Some of the catalogue numbers may be out of date.

SLOANE MS. 307—A collection of Enochian material from other manuscripts.

SLOANE MS. 3190—A copy of the *True Relation* with notes.

BODELEIAN MS. 8465aa (Black Catalogue 580)—*Collation of his printed actions with spirits with the original* MSS. (Ashmole).

BODELEIAN MS. 8460* (Black Catalogue 1788, p 38, 65)—*Papers concerning the actions* (Ashmole).

BODELEIAN MS. 8461* (Black Catalogue 1790, 1-28, 34 &c.)—*Papers concerning the actions* (Ashmole).

BODELEIAN MS. 8462* *Papers concerning the actions* (Ashmole).

BODELEIAN MS. 487 *Notes from his fifth book of Mysteries* (Ashmole).

ASHMOLE MS. 580—Ashmole's copy of *True Relation* with notes and cross references.

ASHMOLE MS. 1788—Various papers relating to the action, compiled by Ashmole.

ASHMOLE MS. 1790—Ashmole's observations and recollections concerning Dee's magical work.

## §4. *Published Works.*

The following published works also contributed to the writing of this volume:—

Meric Casaubon, ed., *A True and Faithful Relation of what passed for many Yeers Between Dr. John Dee and Some Spirits:* London, 1659; Republished by Askin: London, 1974. The published version of Cotton Appendix XLVI Parts 1 & 2.

Aleister Crowley, *The Equinox*, Weiser: New York, 1972, Vol. VIJ, pages 228 to 243 presents some scattered pieces of Sloane MS. 3191 with Golden Dawn elaborations. Volume VIIJ, pages 100-128 presents a 'self-pronouncing' interpretation of the Keys.

John Dee, *The Hieroglyphic Monad*, Weiser: New York, 1975; Dee's early philosophical-magical speculations.

John Dee, *The Mathemitical Præface to the Elements of Geometrie of Euclid of Megara*, Science History Publications: New York, 1975; John Dee's most influential work , but only marginally concerned with magic.

Peter J. French, *John Dee, The World of an Elizabethian Magus*, Routledge and Kegan Paul: London, 1972; A definitive look at Dee's life, including an excellent bibliography of manuscripts and published works about Dee.

James Orchard Halliwell, ed., *The Private Diary of Dr. John Dee*, AMS Press: London, 1968; Another of Dee's diaries, along with a catalogue of the books and manuscripts in his collection prior to its partial destruction.

Donald C. Laycock, *The Complete Enochian Dictionary*, Askin: London, 1978; Contains an accurate transcription of the

Angelical Keys in Sloane MS. 3191, but without pronunciation marks or lacunæ. The English rendering has been
modernized. The dictionary also references Crowley's
'phonetic' Angelical. It includes an excellent bibliography
of recent minor publications dealing with Enochian matters.

Israel Regardie, ed., *The Golden Dawn*, Llewellyn Publications:
St. Paul, 1971; Book Nine contais an overview of then
baroque Golden Dawn 'Enochian' magic, loosely based on
Dee's original system. A version of the Keys is also included.

Leo Vinci, *GMICALZOMA! An Enochian Dictionary*, Regency
Press: London & New York, 1976; An exhaustive early
dictionary.

A. E. Waite, ed., *The Alchemical Writings of Edward Kelly*, Weiser:
New York, 1975; provides a contrast to Kelly's work with
Dee.

CPSIA information can be obtained at www.ICGtesting.com
Printed in the USA
BVOW011719220312

285698BV00001B/8/P

9 781578 634538

Renaissance magician Dr. John Dee developed his groundbreaking
system of Enochian ceremonial magic by channeling angelic spirits
through the body of his associate, Edward Kelly, and recording the
results in a series of notebooks. While Dee received three entire systems
of magic—planetary, zodiacal, and elemental—he never gathered them
together into a single grimoire that would allow another magician to
reproduce his ceremonies.

*The Enochian Evocation* does just that. It puts Dee's magical work into
a form similar to the books of magic that formed Dee's prototypes, and
includes all of Dee's most important notebook, Sloane MS 3191, as well
as the key material from related manuscripts. The result is a coherent
and complete presentation of the Enochian system, along with all rel-
evant magical elements, including two versions (original and corrected)
of the famous Angelical Calls.

Enochian is reputed to be the most powerful of all the systems of magic
and has greatly influenced the work of later occultists like Aleister
Crowley, A.E. Waite, MacGregor Mathers, and Israel Regardie. While
other texts have attempted to build on Dee's work, *The Enochian Evocation* is the only book that presents Dee's complete system of magic as he
intended it to be practiced.

U.S. $19.95

ISBN: 978-1-57863-453-8

51995

9 781578 634538